$20.00

D1478776

AMBUSH

CLYDE BARROW AND BONNIE PARKER IN 1933

AMBUSH

The Real Story of Bonnie and Clyde

by Ted Hinton
as told to Larry Grove

JACKET BY VIC BLACKBURN

SHOAL CREEK PUBLISHERS, INC.

P.O. BOX 9737   AUSTIN, TEXAS 78766

Copyright © 1979 by L. J. Hinton

All rights in this book are reserved. No part of this book may be used or reproduced in any manner whatsoever without a written request to and response from the publisher, except in the case of brief quotations embodied in a review.

First Edition

Lithographed and Bound in the United States of America

Library of Congress Cataloging in Publication Data

Hinton, Ted, 1904–1977.

    Ambush : the real story of Bonnie and Clyde.

    Includes index.

  1. Barrow, Clyde, 1909–1934. 2. Parker, Bonnie, 1910–1934. 3. Crime and criminals—Texas—Biography. I. Grove, Larry, 1923–   II. Title.

HV6245.H48   364.1'55 [B]   79-11686

ISBN 0-88319-041-9

Contents

Illustrations

Foreword

For many years people were after my father, Ted Hinton, to set things straight about the capture of Bonnie and Clyde. He continually resisted. I believe it was his appointment to the Dallas County Historical Commission that finally prompted Ted to write his book. Until then even I couldn't get him to write it, and I tried hard, because of the difference between the legend about the capture and what he told me to be the actual facts.

Ted had told me of a secret agreement between the six officers involved in the capture. This agreement was that the story would remain as it had been written so long as more than one of the officers was living. When it got down to just one surviving officer, regardless of who it was, that man would have the prerogative of leaving history as it was or of telling the real story. Ted was the last surviving officer.

The fact is, these six officers broke the law to capture Bonnie and Clyde. They didn't intend to, but when the chance came unexpectedly, at 4 A.M. on May 23, 1934, to set a trap, they decided that the opportunity to catch the known killers of twelve people outweighed the violation of rights that occurred on that Louisiana road. The trap worked after two years of intensive police work had failed to stop the killing by Bonnie and Clyde. I leave it to readers who follow their trail with Ted to decide if the officers made the right choice.

Ted saw his job as one that had to be done, and he became fascinated with it, even obsessed by it — but he never reduced Clyde and Bonnie to inhuman "cases" in his mind. He had known the Barrow family when he and Clyde were both growing up in Dallas, and he counted Clyde's brothers and parents among his friends. He always admired the guts that made Clyde and Bonnie stand out from the criminals who were such hot copy in the newspapers in the 1930s. The family understood that Ted had to track Clyde down, and in later years Ted helped the family in whatever ways he could.

I knew that Ted was writing a book about his experiences, but I didn't know how it was coming along when he called me on September 23, 1977, and requested that I come over to his place. We discussed some matters that he had going on, and then he dropped his bombshell: he had finished his book.

He handed me the manuscript and all his notes and tapes. At the same time he told me, "Here it is, son. I've finished it, but I won't be able to do anything with it." I told him that we could discuss it further when we went to the D.A.'s luncheon the following Monday, but he said, "I won't be able to make this one. I've got something else that has come up that I've got to do."

I found out what it was that Monday; he had to go into the hospital. Ted died a month later, on October 27, 1977, never having seen his book in print. It stands as his memorial.

L. J. Hinton

L. J. Hinton

Preface

Forty years and more have passed since Ted Hinton and five other peace officers set up an ambush on a lonely road near Gibsland, Louisiana, and ended the lives of the Southwest's most deadly outlaw pair, Bonnie Parker and Clyde Barrow.

In 1977 only Hinton survived of the six officers who were more castigated than praised by many for their trouble. In this book, Hinton tells how it was — and why the officers themselves withheld for so many years some facts about the ambush by mutual agreement. Because part of the story was withheld, some of the legends of Bonnie and Clyde were allowed to grow in a direction that was different from the way it was. Hinton, by the 1970s, saw no harm in setting the record straight for posterity's sake.

Hinton drew not only on newspapers and public records. He kept extensive scrapbooks that preserved letters, check stubs, and many other artifacts from his seventeen-month hunt for Bonnie and Clyde. Mounted in wallpaper catalogs, these records are now on microfilm in the Dallas Public Library. In addition, he kept notebooks full of information about his own personal experience on the trail of the Barrow Gang. And he drew on police sources that were not in the public record to fill in portions of the careers of Bonnie and Clyde. He was a meticulous record keeper — he loved to tell stories, but he always insisted that the facts be straight. In this book the wealth of detail about Bonnie and Clyde testifies to his belief in telling a true story exactly the way it happened.

Officers who were Hinton's contemporaries knew him as a tall and quiet — and fearless — man who was athletic: a baseball player who had professional contract offers from the Cleveland Indian organization, a polo player, a leather-tough rodeo rider. But when Smoot Schmid was elected Sheriff of Dallas County in 1932, to take office on January 1, 1933, Hinton went to work for him to oblige the man who had given him credit on a bicycle he needed as a working youth on the streets of Dallas.

Hinton had worked with the tough and wiry boy gangs who delivered Western Union messages. To work on the streets and resist intimidation by tougher boys required courage and some ability with the fists. (It is a footnote to this true account of the last days of Bonnie and Clyde that the bad boy Clyde Barrow also had been a Western Union messenger for a brief time.)

Sheriff Schmid needed the lanky and tough Hinton ''because Ted knew the town like the back of his hand.'' He also knew the mud-flats called ''The Bog'' that was West Dallas in a time when that section of an otherwise cosmopolitan and fashion-conscious city was spawning grounds for the disenfranchised and the deadly. And none was more deadly than Clyde with Bonnie at his side.

The years have turned the saga of Bonnie and Clyde into a legend so laced with fiction that the modern reader is sure to find surprises in the true account. A motion picture, using dramatic devices, has left the legend at variance with fact in countless places. But the real story is more gripping, though perhaps not nearly so funny. Hinton says there was nothing amusing in the deaths of the dozen people who died of the bandit gang's gunfire, nine officers of the law among them — nor in the sickening deaths of the young lovers murdered in the rain of bullets that cut them down. But Ted Hinton's story is that account that counts: he holds back nothing, even when he was outrun, outsmarted, and weary of a chase that kept him on the road for many, many months.

''People ask me if Clyde and Bonnie could have eluded law enforcement officers today for the many months they eluded my partner Bob Alcorn and me,'' Ted said. ''Not a chance. We had no communications in those days. They could hit a bank and be long gone before we'd hear about it. We could receive radio messages from office to office — but we had no equipment in our cars for receiving or transmitting. Even a telephone call to the next town required help from the central operator.

"Another thing that worked for Bonnie and Clyde: not everybody wanted to see them caught. It was a bad thing, and maybe it still is, that publicity in the newspapers tends to make heroes of people who are unworthy of adulation. I am certain Bonnie and Clyde managed to get as much help eluding us as we ever got when we were trying to track them down."

Hinton admits that he liked Bonnie Parker and saw her as a very pretty young woman with taffy-colored hair that glistened red in the sun and with a complexion that was fair and tended to freckle. "Photographs made with the little box cameras failed to do justice to her looks. The clothes she wore — viewed by later generations — tend to diminish the sparkle she had when I knew her, when she was waiting tables at the restaurant where I used to take my meals. Bonnie could turn heads," Hinton remembers.

In one notable departure from legend, Hinton insists that the picture of Bonnie Parker as a cigar-smoking gun moll was all wrong. Hinton said the cigar picture came about this way: "A photographer in Joplin, Missouri, was given an undeveloped roll of film that had been found in a room that Clyde and Bonnie had occupied. After making some prints, he penned in the cigar for a certain kind of joke. The cigar image was copied and recopied so many times, it became as much a part of Bonnie as her gun." A reference in a newspaper to a "cigar-smoking" companion of Clyde Barrow lent color; a reference to an empty whiskey bottle found at the scene, likewise, was generally fabricated to imply a certain toughness, Hinton claims. "The fact is, Clyde did not drink; Bonnie perhaps drank a little, based on some accounts I have read. But I believe the fact that they *did not* drink was a factor in their success at eluding us. The average badman would eventually give himself away simply through a mistake made when his head wasn't clear. This never happened to Bonnie and Clyde."

As for comparisons with other desperadoes of the period — Machine Gun Kelly, John Dillinger, Pretty Boy Floyd, Alvin Karpis, and others — Hinton believes there is none. "Faced with arrest, they cringed and gave up. So did Raymond Hamilton when I was in a group that arrested him. But Bonnie and Clyde reacted immediately with resistance; they vowed they'd never be taken alive — and, of course, they weren't.''

Anyone who has ever wondered about the character and habits of the Southwest's most famous desperadoes since the frontier gunslinger days will find them in Ted Hinton's book. But the veteran lawman, athlete, and pilot saw Bonnie and Clyde's story primarily as one of the great love stories of the century. ''This is the thing that made them different from the many men and women who found themselves outside the law: they loved each other with an intensity that kept Bonnie Parker at the side of her man — even when she had to know that, at any time, she could have turned herself in and could probably have been freed by sending Clyde to the chair with her testimony. He came to the point of insisting that she do that, but she believed that life without her man would be no life at all. Even when she must have known that Bob Alcorn and I would not rest until we got them — for she knew us that well — she chose to have those remaining weeks or days with Clyde Barrow rather than come in.''

Hinton said he did not relish what he had to do. ''That is the way it had to be,'' he said. ''It was our job to stop them. Six of us fired on them until their bodies were filled with holes. When I opened the car door, Bonnie was gasping for her last breath and died in my arms.''

This book is the saga of Bonnie and Clyde as it was played out at a certain place in a certain time. ''The story,'' Hinton said, ''is impossible to tell without setting it within the framework of what the Southwest was like in the early 1930s when it happened. That was a different time. Bonnie and Clyde were not the only lawbreakers who commanded our attention. It was a period of economic depression and frustration that may have contributed to the lawlessness of the time.''

Let Ted Hinton tell us about Bonnie and Clyde and their times, and how it really was.

LARRY GROVE
Assistant Professor, Journalism
Southern Methodist University

The Story of Bonnie and Clyde
by Bonnie Parker

(This is probably one of several poems Bonnie was writing at
Joplin, Missouri, just before the explosive shootout with police
there on April 13, 1933, which the Barrow Gang
miraculously escaped. A year later Bonnie gave the poems to
her mother at a secret reunion on May 6, 1934, on an East
Dallas county road. *The poem is printed here by kind permission from the Parker Family Archives.)*

> You've read the story of Jesse James—
> Of how he lived and died;
>> If you're still in need
>> Of something to read,
> Here's the story of Bonnie and Clyde.
>
> Now Bonnie and Clyde are the Barrow gang.
> I'm sure you all have read
>> How they rob and steal
>> And those who squeal
> Are usually found dying or dead.
>
> There's lots of untruths to these write-ups;
> They're not so ruthless as that;
>> Their nature is raw;
>> They hate all the law—
> The stool pigeons, spotters, and rats.
>
> They call them cold-blooded killers;
> They say they are heartless and mean;
>> But I say this with pride,
>> That I once knew Clyde
> When he was honest and upright and clean.

But the laws fooled around,
Kept taking him down
And locking him up in a cell,
Till he said to me,
"I'll never be free,
So I'll meet a few of them in hell."

The road was so dimly lighted;
There were no highway signs to guide;
But they made up their minds
If all roads were blind,
They wouldn't give up till they died.

The road gets dimmer and dimmer;
Sometimes you can hardly see;
But it's fight, man to man,
And do all you can,
For they know they can never be free.

From heart-break some people have suffered;
From weariness some people have died;
But take it all in all,
Our troubles are small
Till we get like Bonnie and Clyde.

If a policeman is killed in Dallas,
And they have no clew or guide;
If they can't find a fiend,
They just wipe their slate clean
And hang it on Bonnie and Clyde.

There's two crimes committed in America
Not accredited to the Barrow mob;
They had no hand
In the kidnap demand,
Nor the Kansas City depot job.

A newsboy once said to his buddy:
"I wish old Clyde would get jumped;
    In these awful hard times
    We'd make a few dimes
If five or six cops would get bumped."

The police haven't got the report yet,
But Clyde called me up today;
    He said, "Don't start any fights—
    We aren't working nights—
We're joining the NRA."

From Irving to West Dallas viaduct
Is known as the Great Divide,
    Where the women are kin,
    And the men are men,
And they won't "stool" on Bonnie and Clyde.

If they try to act like citizens
And rent them a nice little flat,
    About the third night
    They're invited to fight
By a sub-gun's rat-tat-tat.

They don't think they're too tough or desperate,
They know that the law always wins;
    They've been shot at before,
    But they do not ignore
That death is the wages of sin.

Some day they'll go down together;
And they'll bury them side by side;
    To few it'll be grief—
    To the law a relief—
But it's death for Bonnie and Clyde.

I

The Dirty Thirties

A DEPUTY'S job paid $150 a month with a $50 car allowance, and I was making more than that at the post office. Only a fool would have thrown aside the security of a government job for a deal like that, especially at that time, in the winter of 1932, after Smoot Schmid had won election as sheriff of Dallas County. A sensible man would know that any man who could win a race for sheriff could also lose and be out of a job again in two short years.

Smoot had won because he was persuasive, and because the previous sheriff hadn't kept up with the working day-to-day business of the office; papers had been slow getting served, expenses had gone up. And all that together made the previous sheriff highly vulnerable for a man like Smoot who had a great many friends.

And, as I said, Smoot was persuasive. I'd helped in his election, putting up a few signs here and there, and talking him up to people I knew. And I suppose I knew as many people in Dallas as anybody.

Where I made my mistake was listening to him when he said he needed me. That's what did it. From the time I was a kid, Smoot had practically raised me. That's a fact. My father was a railroad man, for the Katy, and I wasn't more than five

YOUNG TED HINTON

when my mother told me I wouldn't see him again, that the train had crashed and they'd taken my daddy away. I hadn't known him all that well, but it had to have made an impression.

The long and short of it was that I was on the street early, among the rough element of the town all my young life. When I got a job delivering telegrams for Western Union, it was Smoot who fixed it so I could buy a bike and pay him off at four bits a week from what I'd earn. I must have been all of eleven. I'd hustle the old *Dallas Dispatch* — anything to make a little money. And I'd be around the old Cotton Exchange building at Akard and Wood because the men there would pay me to run errands.

Dallas wasn't large in those days. On a bike, a kid could know it from one end to the other: the silk-stocking areas out near the university, in Highland Park, and the older settled area in East Dallas, where some very rich people lived, and across the Trinity River in West Dallas where poor whites and the thugs hung out. The black people lived in South Dallas then. I lived across the river in Oak Cliff, which was about the middle so far as income levels and status was concerned. It was in Oak Cliff, near the river, that the old Dallas Steers of the Texas League played baseball. I'd try to make time to see some baseball. But between all my jobs, the only time I had to spare would find me playing in the old city sandlot leagues. Still, I had a pretty fair time as a boy.

It wasn't that I didn't cotton to the other boys at Western Union, but it hadn't taken long to see that the other street urchins who took those jobs could get a fellow into a mess of trouble. When they'd pair off, one kid would knock on a front door to deliver a wire or ask a direction while his buddy was ransacking something out back that could be peddled for pocket change. I never squealed on any of them; that wasn't my style. But I never backed down from a fight either. Several times, I probably *should* have backed down, but then I didn't do it.

I remember one of the photographs of those days — thirty-seven Western Union delivery boys on their bikes, all in a row. Twelve were to go to prison and four would be electro-

LOOKING TOUGH IN THE DALLAS OF 1922: TED AND HIS FRIENDS (INCLUDING CURTIS HAMBLIN, GLOVER FUNDERBURK, AND ECK MINYARD, LEFT TO RIGHT ABOVE) HUNG OUT AT SMOOT SCHMID'S CYCLE COMPANY AT 315 N. AKARD. LIKE TED, HAMBLIN WAS A WESTERN UNION MESSENGER AND MINYARD WORKED AT THE POST OFFICE.

cuted. Not right then. But later, when their sorry small crimes turned into murder and things like that.

All of that learning the town was a help when I went for the post office job. I don't think it hurt, either, that I was a fair baseball player. It was important at the post office that the ball club did well in the City League. When the Cleveland Indians offered me a chance to turn professional, after we'd won a couple of city championships, I thought seriously about that. But I had a wife — had one since I was eighteen — and the post office job just made more sense.

But going to work as a deputy sheriff under Smoot Schmid made no sense at all. "Hell, Smoot," I reasoned with him, "I don't want to arrest anybody."

All he said was "I need you, Ted, and you'll do fine. What I'll have you on," he said, stretching the truth somewhat, "is process serving. You'll be able to find all these people, knowing where they live and all. And don't worry about that 'job security' — I'll be sheriff forever."

On January 1, 1933, I became officially a reluctant deputy sheriff. That same afternoon, I was walking back to the office on the first floor of Dallas's old red courthouse after lunch and there was a fellow with a pistol in his belt, a machete in his hand, and a glassy look in his eyes. I introduced myself and told him I'd have to take that wicked-looking machete and that pistol. Damned if he didn't give them up and accompany me back to the jail for someone else to decide if he was a criminal or just crazy. Sometimes there's such a fine line.

I was lucky. He came without resistance. I have always been lucky.

Ted Hinton, age twenty-seven, in 1931, two years before he began his search for Bonnie and Clyde

II

Ante Up

EVEN THOUGH Smoot assured me I'd be serving papers for the sheriff's office, he intended for me to get my feet wet in law enforcement. And it made sense to me to learn as much as I could about everything that was going on, the dice games, the prostitution, the pawn shops that were taking the stuff the burglars stole. From the time he offered the job to me, I began observing Dallas and the whole county with a lawman's point of view of the trouble spots.

One of Dallas's major troublemakers in the early 1930s was Clyde Barrow. By the time I became a deputy sheriff, he was wanted for four murders. I knew him fairly well, though not so well as I knew his father and mother, Henry and Cumie, or his older brother, Ivan, whom we all called "Buck." His father couldn't read or write, but quietly he seemed to be a decent and hard-working man, not long off the farm. It was well known around Dallas that Clyde had gone off with Bonnie Parker and that they had been sweethearts since the first time he met her in 1930. I had become friends with Bonnie when she served my meals at the old American Cafe, where most of the post office people ate lunch, alongside the three-story Texas Hotel. It was across the street from a black-smith shop in those days. A bit later, the post office annex would be built there.

Long before it ever became a matter of law enforcement business, Bonnie would tell me about herself. She was born down at Rowena, Texas, in 1910 and had spent some vacations with kinfolk in the little Oklahoma mining towns of Commerce and Picher. She always said she'd have liked being a singer, or maybe a poet, and she used to sing when she was in school at Cement City, west of Dallas. Bonnie was perky, with good looks and taffy-colored hair that showed a trace of red, and she had some freckles. She always had a ready quip, too. She must have been a good student, for she had won a spelling bee when she was in school. I couldn't imagine her having any criminal record; she was such a tiny girl — couldn't have weighed a hundred pounds. She had married a schooldays chum named Roy Thornton when she was just fifteen or sixteen, and they had parted over something or other. A little after that, Thornton was caught in a robbery and was sent to do some time in prison. Bonnie never did divorce him. She just said, ''it wouldn't be right.''

Several of the men my age flirted with her, and Bonnie could turn off the advances or lead a customer on with her easy conversation. I'm sure she must have been seeing Clyde on occasion at the cafe, but I have no memory of seeing the two of them together there.

Clyde was the fourth in a family of eight that Henry and Cumie Barrow brought into the world. Clyde was born at Teleco, near Ennis, southeast of Dallas, in 1909. Like so many other families on farms in that time, the Barrows moved into Dallas to get away from the drudgery of farm work and the lack of opportunity that farming presented to anyone who didn't own a piece of land. Old Man Barrow and his wife already were showing signs of being old when they weren't really old at all.Weary might have been a better word for them, and I knew them well enough to know how it came about.

The Barrow boys got a name early as ''that Barrow Bunch.'' They were in scrapes a lot of the time. And there were enough of them that only a fool would dare to cross any member of the family. Buck, the oldest of the four boys, never made the ''Most Wanted'' list, but he set the early path that Clyde followed and outdid. The troubles of the rest of the family stemmed from things they did out of loyalty to Clyde and Buck.

Henry and Cumie still would get occasional visits from their sons, even now that the boys had turned to a life of full-time crime. At their station on old West Dallas Road (now paved and called Singleton Boulevard), Henry and Cumie would take turns serving customers at the gas pumps where either the red or white Sims Gas could be bought (thirteen cents a gallon for the red, twelve cents for the white). Inside there were a few grocery items in cans. The soft-drink cooler offered Coca Cola and red soda pop, and the meat cooler kept a supply of lunch meat or rolls of bologna, what we called in those days "South Dallas Round Steak." To their customers in West Dallas, the Barrows seemed as normal as anyone else. But if you wear a heavy heart long enough, it is going to show.

Clyde had been hauled in for chicken theft — and so had older brother Buck, who enjoyed the violence of cockfighting. The next step — car theft — came in 1926 when Clyde took a car for a spin around before abandoning it.

In those days, for a first offense, it was the custom to have the parents bring the boy in. With a fatherly talk from the judge, parents would have an opportunity to follow up with whatever punishment they deemed proper to impress upon the boy that crime would not pay.

"One thing always led to another," his father Henry confided to me more than once. Henry was never talkative, but he seemed to enjoy my stopping to chat, before and after I joined the sheriff's department. "I've tried to talk some sense into his head," he would say. "A working man just don't have time to sit on his kids all the time. And he's really not *all* bad, Ted," he'd tell me. I wasn't so much older than Clyde myself.

There were four additional arrests for suspected auto theft before Clyde came to the serious attention of police. He was known as "one of the Barrow Boys," a term that signified no-accounts.

Arrested for auto theft in Waco, a hundred miles south of Dallas, Clyde gave his name as "Elvin Williams" — and no one tied the name to the Clyde Barrow who had a juvenile record for car theft in Dallas. When he came well dressed to court and pleaded for mercy, the elders on the jury were impressed and refused to convict him.

By the time he was twenty-one, in 1930, Clyde had met Bonnie, who was waiting tables at the American Cafe. Lacking money to buy things to impress her, he took to burglary. Cars impressed Bonnie, and no one enjoyed driving like the wind more than Clyde, nor could anyone drive so fast or so well as Clyde with Bonnie at his side.

During the first week of March, 1930, the District Court of McLennan County at Waco sentenced Clyde to fourteen years in the state penitentiary — two years each on separate counts of stealing five cars and burglaries of two Waco business houses. But Clyde didn't languish long in jail. Bonnie came to visit him and was told of a house that contained a gun. Would she go to the house and return the gun to him in the jail? Bonnie agreed to try. She left and returned the same afternoon with the gun, then returned to the house and waited for Clyde and his cell mate to pick her up for a ride back to Dallas.

The boys made the break but did not return for her. She hitchhiked back to Dallas. Clyde was picked up a few days later in Middleton, Ohio, and returned once more to Waco to await his turn being admitted to the state prison at Huntsville.

The modern reader may be puzzled at the thought that there was no room in the penitentiary for anyone sentenced to serve fourteen years — but that was the case for a time in 1930. The Texas prison system had about 75,000 acres of land at various farms, and more hardened felons were kept at "The Walls" at the main prison in Huntsville. Prisoners farmed the land or cut timber to defray costs of their incarceration. There had been abuses in the system before; wardens and prison employees rented prisoners to work on the private farms of people willing to make a payoff. Under a succession of governors, paroles and pardons seemed to be given for a price, and prison reform had been a campaign issue in the biennial race for governor. As recently as 1925, investigations had proved that prison guards were using the "bat" and the lash to punish malingerers and troublemakers inside the prison.

The press clamored for reform, but public opinion did not come easily to the side of the convicts; they were there, after all, to be punished — and they were eating regularly, something that not everyone on the outside could accomplish during the Depression years. Still, conditions were intolerable. On March 25, 1930, Lee Simmons of Sherman, Texas, was hired to manage the prison system, to make it as self-sustaining as possible, and to make such reforms as he saw fit. And until Simmons had an opportunity to effect some reorganization, Governor Dan Moody said there'd simply be no more prisoners admitted to the state prison system. The county jails would just have to hold them.

A month after Lee Simmons took over, the freeze on admittance was lifted. Clyde Barrow was given number 63527 by the Texas prison system and began serving his sentence on April 21, 1930. He listed his wife as "Bonnie" — a small lie, but a way of making it possible to receive letters from her. He listed his date of birth correctly as March 24 but gave the year as 1912 (which would have made him eighteen) rather than the truthful answer, 1909. He said he had seven years schooling, and he listed his occupation (from a job he had held at United Glass Company in Dallas) as glazier. Examination showed his height to be 5'5½'', weight 127 pounds, eyes brown, complexion medium fair, and hair dark chestnut (which perhaps accounts for the middle name of Chestnut that the family gave him. But he gave his middle name to prison interviewers as "Champion.") He wore a heart and dagger tattoo and the initials EBW (for his alias, Elvin Williams) on the outer part of his left forearm. A shield with the letters USN was tattoed on the inner part of his right forearm — presumably for the U. S. Navy, though Clyde never served in the navy. Another tattoo on the outer side of his arm bore a picture of a girl's head. The admission slip noted that he wore a size six shoe. And to the questions, "Do you smoke, drink, or gamble?" Clyde had replied, "No."

There was no reason at that time for anyone in an official position to notice Barrow. Certainly many prisoners could have been labeled as more dangerous than he. Not much concern was wasted on a fuzzy-cheeked car thief.

Barrow was assigned to Eastham Prison Farm, about forty miles north of Huntsville, near Crockett, at the edge of what we in Texas call the East Texas Piney Woods. Modern penologists have high praise for programs that allow the prisoner to get his outdoor exercise. And farm work, while strenuous to anyone who has led a soft life in town, is seldom back breaking.

Nevertheless, convicts had a dislike for anything that smacked of work. And there was one way that had been used by some prisoners to win a transfer to the soft life in a barred room at the Walls — and more than a few took the route to win some time eating better food in the prison hospital. Clyde Barrow was one who coaxed a fellow prisoner into bringing the sharp and heavy steel blade of an ax down on two of his toes. A certain paleness of face results; there is a gush of blood and some immediate pain. But that, too, would end after a time. And with two toes missing, the field work would be behind him for at least a few weeks.

What Clyde really wanted, I learned later, was a transfer back to the main lockup at Huntsville. Some convicts had beat the system this way. If, in the act of defiance, there was a life-long disfigurement that had to be an inconvenience, it might appear totally sensible to a man in prison whose mind does not work exactly as yours works. But even that obvious act to get himself assigned to the Walls, away from farm work and wood-cutting, failed to win sympathy or a transfer for Clyde. He remained at Eastham Farm until February of 1932, when he returned to Dallas with a parole in his hands.

III

Murder Begins

THE CROWDED penitentiary system and the prevailing opinion in a time of economic depression that prisoners ought to pay for their own upkeep or be forced out to make their own way made the parole a popular action in the early 1930s. Some paroles were warranted and worked to the benefit of everyone. Clyde Barrow's parole was one of the famous mistakes.

Clyde's mother, Cumie Barrow, and his sisters prevailed on Governor Ross Sterling to sign Clyde's parole. This surely took Clyde by surprise, since he had had his toes axed only a few weeks before. He was wearing crutches when he came home from prison.

Clyde came back in a suit the prison gave him, but he shed it soon. He was determined to become a well-dressed dandy. His family sensed that Clyde had changed; he said he intended to wear silk shirts and buy some kid gloves. Somehow that was a signal to the plain, hard-working family that prison life had left Clyde harder and more cynical. Shirts of silk, they believed, were favored only by gangsters, pimps, and bootleggers.

If the forced absence of almost two years had changed anything between Clyde and his girl friend Bonnie, it only increased their fondness for each other. Clyde was Bonnie's man.

She urged him then, as she had urged him in lonely letters written to him in prison, to give up his "fast" life and get a regular job. There surely were places Clyde could get a job. But where?

Clyde's sister offered to help. She had a friend who knew a man in Worcester, Massachusetts, in the construction business. A job in Massachusetts seemed made to order. It would allow Clyde what he said he wanted — "some place where people won't be looking over my shoulder, won't look cross-eyed at me because I'm a con, or one of the Barrow Boys." Clyde found money enough to take a train to Massachusetts. Not for the ticket; he would make his way there on a freight. But it never hurt anything to have pocket money.

There is nothing in the record that would indicate that Clyde did anything wrong in Massachusetts. Nor anything particularly right, either. He was homesick, for Bonnie, for people he knew, for his old haunts. Within two weeks, his sister was receiving letters that told her Clyde wasn't really getting on with the job. He was restless. By the middle of March, the episode of Clyde Barrow going straight was finished. He headed home to Dallas, where people didn't talk funny and where he could whistle up some action among his friends.

Bonnie resigned at the American Cafe and joined Clyde. Her mother saw nothing unusual in her absence. Bonnie told her she had been offered a better job in Houston, showing cosmetics for a company that promised she could make more money than she could make waiting tables. "And I won't be depending on the tips," Bonnie told her. Bonnie had a good head on her, Mrs. Parker told anyone who inquired. She was in Houston and that was that. But Bonnie was sparing her mother the truth.

On a lark, they found a young operator named Raymond Hamilton, a slight and pale blond-haired youth who had settled in Dallas from Wichita Falls to the west. Raymond was, like so many hellers his age, a "hip pocket" bootlegger. In a time when it was unlawful to sell whiskey, a bootlegger could produce a flask for a price. Sometimes, *most* times, it was homemade, the product of someone who had a still hidden somewhere and could run off a batch of illegal whiskey that was called by various names: redeye, white lightning, moonshine, rotgut, or simply booze. In a time when a used car could be bought for thirty dollars, and white gas could be bought ''on credit'' from Clyde's father's station, there was nothing to keep the boys from running around and having their adventures.

Cars were easy enough to steal; Clyde and Ray could always find one to use and discard when they found another. But once, near Kaufman, a town east of Dallas, a victim of one of their planned robberies balked at handing over his money. They hurried to the car in which Bonnie was waiting and eluded their pursuers for a time by heading the car down a country lane. Very soon, the car was hopelessly bogged and stuck in mud from a recent rain. Still they ran, trying even to make a getaway on a pair of mules they spotted in a field. But the mules balked, too. They took cover in a ditch, waiting for the local peace officers to give up their search and for night to fall.

Bonnie on that occasion was told to make her way to an abandoned country church and to wait until the boys could circle back to the town and steal another car. Then they'd come for her. But she waited through a long night, with no sight of Clyde and Ray. By morning, she walked to the main highway and waited for a passerby to offer a ride. But the first offer came from a law enforcement man. Bonnie was taken to the Kaufman jail for questioning.

She was not fingerprinted. To the best of my knowledge, she was never fingerprinted as long as she lived. She was kept in the jail, treated as a favored prisoner, and no one outside Kaufman's police department was aware of her presence. During the day, apparently, she passed the time with the police chief's wife. The only reason the incident of the Kaufman jail is pertinent at all to the story of Bonnie and Clyde is that she spoke of it later to a member of the family who repeated it to me: Bonnie was thoroughly ''mad'' at Clyde and Ray for abandoning her and not returning to pick her up before they fled. She swore she'd never go out again with Clyde.

On March 25, Clyde and Ray held up the manager of the Sims Oil Company at the company's Dallas headquarters and got a handfull of bills before fleeing. Both were identified from photos.

Bonnie still was living out her confinement at Kaufman when Clyde and Ray drove to a little Mom-and-Pop station on the outskirts of Hillsboro on the night of April 23, 1932. Clyde had been there before, inquiring whether the proprietors, J. N. Bucher and his wife, Martha, would buy some fine carving knives he took "in a trade." At that time the Buchers admired the knives but decided against buying them.

On the night of the twenty-third, Clyde and Ray rapped on the front door and set up a racket until Bucher came to an upstairs window. "It's me: the boy who tried to sell you the knives. Will you open up. We gotta get some guitar strings. Been down to a dance, and the guitar busted. Won't take a minute."

In a short time, Bucher came downstairs and admitted Clyde and Ray. He snapped on the light and Clyde handed him a ten-dollar bill. He already had spotted the guitar strings, which he picked from a display card, and waited. It is merely speculation, but Clyde surely had noticed the safe at the rear of the store when he brought the knives.

"Got anything smaller?" Bucher asked him. Barrow said he didn't, and Bucher said he'd have to call his wife down to unlock the safe. The boys surely had not expected this turn of events; now they would be spotted by two victims instead of only one.

Ray pulled a gun as Bucher knelt to open the safe. In a flash a shell exploded against the safe; Mrs. Bucher screamed; and Bucher slumped to the floor — the bullet had ricocheted from the safe to strike Bucher in the heart.

Clyde and Ray dashed for the front door without waiting to claim any of the money from the open safe, without even taking back the ten-dollar bill.

Mrs. Bucher bent over her fatally wounded husband and heard a car speed away, churning up gravel from the drive as it dug in for the getaway.

The morning would bring an investigation, but the leads were scant. Modern police methods and communications may have made the crime simple to solve. In 1932, the task was not so easy. Peace officers could have their suspicions and their hunches that the young men Mrs. Bucher described were Clyde Barrow and Raymond Hamilton — but a hundred such "suspects" might also fit her description. Even when she picked out Clyde's photograph as the youth who accompanied the young man with the gun when it discharged and killed her husband, there was no certainty that a conviction would have grown out of the evidence.

But for Clyde Barrow and Raymond Hamilton — particularly Clyde — the fact of Clyde's presence at a murder while he was only paroled from prison was enough to bring him to a serious question: should he stay on the run? Or should he give himself up and face what he was certain in his mind would bring a conviction and, quite probably, the electric chair? Barrow chose not to give up.

As for Bonnie's promise never to go out with Clyde again, the love affair blossomed just as soon as Bonnie was no longer under the watchful eye of the jailers at Kaufman. When the grand jury met, on June 17, there was no evidence to hold her; the case against her was dropped, and she was allowed to go free. Dallas didn't see much of Bonnie after that; she was "out." She was with Clyde. And Clyde — people in West Dallas agreed — was "going to get himself into a mess of trouble if he isn't careful."

Purely in a sense of being neighborly, for I had no intention of ever becoming a peace officer, I had talked with Henry Barrow about his boys. But Henry would only shake his head; I doubt that the old man knew the extent Clyde was outdoing even his brother Buck. And I am positive that no one in the world could have convinced Bonnie's mother that the girl who was constantly being identified as the pretty auburn-haired accomplice on so many robberies was her daughter.

Clyde Barrow was not yet "notorious" when he was paroled from prison; he had been considered one of the West Dallas "bad boys" — one of several dozens who bore some watching, so far as the machinery of justice was concerned. But not much more.

In my opinion, in early 1932 he still could have turned back and "gone straight" — possibly even after the Hillsboro shooting on April 23. But his family told me, even at that time, that they worried about him every waking minute. And that Clyde was convinced already that if he were ever captured, after what the law had accused him of doing while he was on parole from prison, his life would be snuffed out — "like Lottie's eye."

Considering that Clyde believed that — and had a taste of ego that convinced him he could be a "big man" so long as he had guns and the mobility that any stolen car could bring him — it is no great surprise that he set about living a part. Having a good-looking woman by his side, a woman who would be noticed in any crowd, a woman who adored him — all this only spurred him to be more cunning and daring than ever.

On July 16, 1932, a young bookkeeper named Roy Evans was abducted from his office at the Palestine Ice Company in East Texas, forced by a pair of bandits to drive them to a spot outside of town. He was beaten and robbed of $989.

On July 27, two young bandits robbed the First State Bank of Willis, Texas, in Montgomery County. C. A. Johnson, the bank manager, and L. R. Paddock, the cashier, gave up something over three thousand dollars — and they still were locked in a vault as the bandits sped away. Townspeople had to dig a hole in the side of the bank to release them.

Descriptions of the robbers fit Clyde Barrow, Raymond Hamilton, and the ever-present girl who waited in a car outside, Bonnie Parker.

At 10 A. M. Friday, July 29, a pair of young bandits — later identified positively as Clyde Barrow and Raymond Hamilton — found manager C. H. Spears alone in the Interurban Rail Station at Grand Prairie, twelve miles west of Dallas. At gunpoint, the fifty-two-year-old station keeper was forced to lie on his back while the bandits rifled his cash drawer. They got only twelve dollars this time before fleeing in what everyone agreed was a "sporty high-powered roadster."

On August 1 they staged a daylight hijacking of the Neuhoff Packing Company plant office in Dallas, getting just under five hundred dollars. Radios were blaring the news that the bandits were "believed to be Clyde Barrow and Raymond

Hamilton.'' They were now gaining notoriety — and again they seemed to disappear into thin air.

It is part of the record now that these were all their escapades. After the packing plant job, they picked up Bonnie and later in the week were in the hills of eastern Oklahoma to await their next escapade.

As the city of Dallas was readying a grand welcome home for Mildred ''Babe'' Didrikson, who had overwhelmed her opposition in the 1932 Olympic Games, Clyde, Bonnie, and Raymond Hamilton were looking for their excitement wherever they could find it. On Friday evening, August 5, they barged in on a roadside dance at the little Oklahoma country town of Stringtown near the old Indian capitol at Atoka.

Later that same evening, witnesses recalled the splash that Bonnie had been making, dancing first with Clyde and then with Raymond, whirling around in her bright red dress — and easily the prettiest girl in the place.

But trouble started when they stopped dancing. Instead of returning to their own car, the three slid into a car nearer the dance-hall door. On this evening, they passed around a fruit jar filled with potent moonshine whiskey — ''white lightning'' it is called in the southeastern Oklahoma hills still known today as ''Little Dixie.''

One local youth, who had been rebuffed by Bonnie and told to ''shove off'' by her men friends, asked help from local lawmen to have them removed from his car so he could leave.

Sheriff C. G. Maxwell and his deputy E. C. Moore appeared to inquire about the mix-up. This wasn't the type of thing that one would expect to lead to violence. ''What's going on here?'' Moore asked the strangers.

The boys answered with a volley of gunfire. A pistol shot entered Moore's forehead and he fell dead. Maxwell fired and received fire from the fleeing troublemakers. He was critically wounded but did not die.

In the next few days officers of Oklahoma and Texas were alerted. A suspect named Dyer was picked up; he admitted having ridden to the dance with the other suspects but said he remained at the dance hall when ''all hell broke loose'' and others were running around in a state of hysteria.

Dyer tried to be a helpful witness. He remembered that Barrow had told him he had relatives in Dallas and "not hell or high water, nor the Law" could keep him from seeing them any time he took the notion — even if he had to shoot his way in. Clyde was developing his famous boldness.

While roadblocks were set at all northern approaches into Dallas for the next few days, something of the movements of the fugitives began to filter in, and the information was pieced together.

They had changed automobiles a half dozen times and had left them abandoned. Once Bonnie feigned illness, and they lured a farmer to take them in his car to "get this sick woman to a hospital." When the farmer started his car, he was slugged and thrown out, and the people he had befriended drove his car away.

Already the threesome was becoming elusive. Clyde seemed to know every highway and every back road in Oklahoma, Louisiana, and Texas.

But he wasn't my problem — at least not yet. I didn't realize, in the hot summer of 1932, that I was moving into a head-on course with Clyde and Bonnie. I was busy helping my friend Preacher Hays get Smoot Schmid elected sheriff — though politics never was my game either. Smoot led the voting in a three-man race in the Democratic Party primary. But the election laws in Texas called for the two leaders to engage in a "runoff" race. And as the final tallies were made, I remember feeling satisfied that Smoot Schmid had won with his campaign to run a "businesslike" sheriff's office.

Clyde and Bonnie were to be much larger names in the crime world before Smoot and his new force of deputies, myself included, would be sworn into office on January 1, 1933.

IV

No Turning Back

THE AFFAIR at the roadside dance hall was the point of no turning back in the careers of Clyde Barrow and Raymond Hamilton. Bonnie, of course, could have gone home and, quite probably, taken back her old job at the American Cafe with few questions asked. But now the needless shooting of the two Oklahoma officers had riled law enforcement people everywhere. Even so, with Clyde's finesse at driving and knowing the road off the pavement and Raymond's talent for stealing cars, they were difficult to catch. They ran a series of roadblocks, eluding police completely, and even returned to Dallas for a visit with their families.

But resuming their old life of knocking around Dallas without fear of arrest was out of the question. Bonnie had an aunt who lived near Carlsbad, New Mexico, so the three drove out to see her. The aunt, Millie Stamps, was unaware when they drove into the dirt driveway that either her niece Bonnie or her friends were in any sort of trouble.

On Sunday morning, Ray took a ride into town to buy a block of ice for some hand-churned ice cream. Deputy Sheriff Joe Johns had seen the strange license plate before; when he spotted it again, he tailed the car back to the Stamps house.

There may always be some doubt that this is precisely what happened. Mrs. Stamps later denied she called out the sheriff when she became suspicious of Bonnie's friends — but she could never be certain the boys believed that.

When Johns knocked on the door to inquire about the car — to see if it matched one that had been reported stolen — Bonnie answered the door. "The boys will be out in a minute. They're dressing," she said.

Johns returned to the car and may have seen some of the arsenal of weapons that were carried half covered in the back seat. But by then it was too late for comment. Though the boys had been careful to leave their weapons locked in the car to avoid their being seen by Bonnie's aunt, they must have thought it opportune that a hunting weapon — a shotgun — was in the house. They emerged from the back door and had the weapon trained on the sheriff before he was aware.

"Nice and easy, or I'll blow your head off," Barrow said.

Johns dropped his weapon. A shotgun blast resounded loudly. It was accidental and hit nobody.

"Hurry it up in there, Bonnie," Clyde yelled, and slid the key into the lock of the car door. "Hold it on him, Ray," Clyde said. And he started the car. Bonnie came running out of the house.

"Let's take him with us," Clyde said. And Johns found himself an unwilling passenger in the Barrow car. It was making dust as it headed out, and Mrs. Stamps knew she must report what had happened. But again there would be no chance to overtake Clyde and Ray and Bonnie. The telephone wires were busy, alerting the law enforcement offices for miles around. But the sheriff had been kidnapped.

Something of Clyde's ability to drive long distances without letup can be guessed at with the knowledge that the car pulled out of Carlsbad shortly before noon — and there still was some summer daylight at 8 P. M. when Sheriff Johns telephoned wearily from San Antonio, several hundred miles away, to his office in Carlsbad, saying that he was tired but unharmed. Clyde's driving time was extraordinary considering that highways were not so wide then and that he frequently left the main road during the kidnap flight. Johns said he was exhausted, but his captors appeared exhilarated. The following morning they abandoned that car in Victoria, some distance to the southeast and toward the Texas coast, stole another one, and headed toward Houston in a northeastern direction.

So hot were they now that a roadblock was set up at a bridge leading over the Colorado River at Wharton. This time, the officers swore, they'd be ready. They were to learn — as so many of us were to learn later — that Clyde Barrow was a difficult man to outguess. At the approach to the bridge, only Clyde and Bonnie appeared in the Ford coupe that approached — and the officers had been notified from Victoria that they would quite likely approach in a V-8 sedan. Clyde had figured this in advance; the coupe had been stolen — and Hamilton was driving behind them in a sedan.

At the approach, Clyde wheeled around in the road to the astonishment of the ambush laying in wait at the approach to the bridge. He fired as he wheeled and received a hail of fire from the lawmen as he passed Raymond approaching. Raymond turned around, too, somehow being missed by every shot that was fired. He gathered up Clyde and Bonnie and all three escaped in the direction they had been coming.

One officer had been slightly wounded. Another charge would be lodged against the outlaw threesome, but that hardly mattered now.

Events were piling up, and they were making some areas of the country dangerous for Clyde, Bonnie, and Ray. After a few more small jobs, Hamilton decided that he could take some time to enjoy life — he would simply head out on his own in a part of the country where no one knew him. He might even visit his father, whom he hadn't seen for a long time, in Michigan.

Hamilton picked up with another West Dallas outlaw named Gene O'Dare, who had been making his way in small-time bootlegging and minor thievery. O'Dare had recently married a girl named Mary in Wichita Falls; but that was no problem. He left her and joined Hamilton for some partying in Michigan. Clyde and Bonnie would have no trouble finding other partners from West Dallas for companionship when they needed it.

On October 11, the lean old butcher Howard Hall was about to close the neighborhood grocery he worked for the Littles at Wells and Vaden Streets in Sherman, across the street from what was then St. Vincent's Hospital. Homer Glaze, a store clerk, watched as a two-door Ford drove up and a well-dressed young man got out and walked into the store, going directly to the meat counter.

Bonnie was parked outside; she had scooted under the wheel of the car. Inside, Barrow ordered bologna, "about a half pound," and "a few slices of cheese." Hall turned to slice the bologna and heard Glaze say, "What is this?" The butcher turned to see Glaze staring into the barrel of a pistol Barrow held on him. "Your money. Give it to me," Barrow ordered. The crusty old butcher came dashing from behind the counter, meat cleaver in hand, as Glaze handed Barrow a handful of bills. The butcher swung at Barrow, and Barrow fired, backing away as Hall continued swinging the cleaver and forcing Barrow toward the south door. Barrow pumped another shot into the old butcher's chest, and he fell in a pool of his own blood, gasping for breath. Barrow made his way to the waiting car that Bonnie already had set in motion; they drove west on Wells Street and north on Hazelwood to make their escape.

Another employee, Lester Butler, came running from behind the store to see the car pulling away; the wife of the owner, Mrs. Little, heard the gunshot in her house next door to the neighborhood store and came running out. Her husband had just brought most of the day's receipts to the house before the stickup occurred. The bandit pair had netted only about twenty-eight dollars; another ten dollars in change was left in the cash register.

Hall, who might have bluffed someone less desperate, died trying to stop Clyde Barrow. He was rushed across the street to the hospital but expired in an elevator on the way to surgery.

Clyde and Bonnie vanished into Oklahoma and Missouri, committing small robberies — some of them with a new pair of running partners, Hollis Hale and Frank Hardy of Dallas. At Oronogo, Missouri, Bonnie went in to case the bank, and a few days later the three men hit it; but Bonnie's visit had put the bank employees on the alert. When Clyde and Hardy went in to pull off the job, leaving Hollis at the getaway car, the robbery was barely under way when bank employees began to rush the pair. They emerged with a sackful of money and ran for their lives.

The division of spoils is said to have broken up the partnership. In any case, afterwards Clyde and Bonnie were alone again in their spree. Their families later heard of one bank they visited in another town, where a gray-haired old man sat disconsolately in a corner of the bank.

To Barrow's command, "this is a stickup," the old man merely grinned.

"What's the matter? What's so damned funny?" Barrow barked.

"I'll tell you what's funny," the old man said. "This bank's been shut down for four days. There ain't no money. That's what's funny . . . ."

Clyde and Bonnie made their way back to Dallas and found W. D. Jones eager to join them on their next outing. W. D. was a mere boy of sixteen, but he had known Clyde almost all his life. He idolized the bandit.

To Clyde's admonition that he'd only get into trouble, W. D. said he was constantly in trouble anyway — and he'd like to get in on some of the action. That was the first week in December, 1932. When Clyde and Bonnie headed south, young W. D. was with them.

At Temple, in Central Texas, salesman Doyle Johnson had just purchased a new car for his wife. In their cruise around Belton, Clyde spotted the car and told W. D. he could be initiated into the gang by stealing it. There was one small problem; W. D. wasn't familiar with all makes of cars. He couldn't get the car started. Clyde ran to assist, but Johnson came running, too — grabbing Clyde's arm and clinging to it. In an instant, Clyde fired his pistol; Johnson was sent reeling, a bullet through his head.

Bonnie wheeled the Barrow Ford alongside; Clyde got in, and W. D., thoroughly scared, flung himself in the back seat. The first taste of crime with Clyde and Bonnie had been bungled. W. D. wouldn't have been missed yet in Dallas, and he returned home. Clyde and Bonnie had to lay low for awhile. They had chalked up their fourth victim.

WANTED BY SHERIFF,DALLAS,TEXAS
         For Bank Robbery
RAYMOND HAMILTON,DALLAS,TEXAS,#10661
     Age 19 (1932). Ht.5-6½ S
Wt 138. Hair Blonde. Eyes Blue.
     Complex. Med. Bld.Slender.

F.P.C.   8 1 Ua 16
          1 1 U 17

RAYMOND HAMILTON GRADUATED TO MAJOR CRIME WHEN HE MET
CLYDE BARROW.

V

The Hamilton Connection

AS THE New Year of 1933 broke, I checked in early at the sheriff's office at the Dallas County Courthouse, my first day on a job I hadn't really wanted. A headline in the afternoon *Dallas Times Herald* said, "Whoopee greets new year with passing of unpopular 1932." The newspaper said there was hope that the economy would get better, that it could hardly get worse. The new sheriff, my new boss, Smoot Schmid, said he would keep fifty-seven deputies — five more than his predecessor Hal Hood had — but he still would cut the total payroll to $80,000 from the $90,000 in effect the year before. There was belt tightening all around. The Tax Assessor Ed Cobbs asked the County Commissioners to cut county taxes by 20 percent. Even the state of Texas was cutting back the state budget by almost $15 million, leaving a budget of $38 million. That wouldn't leave much money for law enforcement or anything else, at a time when crime was running rampant throughout the Southwest.

I met all the deputies again; I already knew most of them. Smoot kept most of the men who had been working for the previous sheriff. He would have been a fool not to have kept some of the outstanding ones, like Bob Alcorn. Alcorn was respected by everybody in town; he was cool, quiet, and he wasn't afraid of anybody. I'd been fishing and hunting with him, and he could shoot with the best of them. But Alcorn was on the criminal division side of the sheriff's operation; and I hired out for the civil division. My job was to serve subpoenas.

It wasn't long until Smoot was having me and my partner, John Hays, look in on gambling operations. We knew where they were; in time, we broke them up, but they'd set up operation in another place. Even some of the process serving was adventurous.

One businessman whose office was in one of the taller buildings simply was eluding us, yet we had to serve him papers. John knocked on his door, and he kept it locked. But John kept him detained until I could walk on a ledge and enter the office through a window high above the city streets. The newspapers made more of the danger than the escapade deserved, but we found one surprised individual when I jumped in through a window.

By the time I joined the force, Clyde Barrow was wanted for four murders: the shooting of J. N. Bucher at Hillsboro on April 23, 1932; the shooting of Deputy E. C. Moore at Atoka, Oklahoma, on August 5, 1932; the murder of Howard Hall in the Sherman, Texas, grocery on October 11, 1932; and, most recently, the December 5, 1932, shooting of salesman Doyle Johnson at Temple, Texas. Further, he had wounded two other deputies, one at Atoka, Oklahoma, and another at Wharton, Texas; he had kidnapped Sheriff Joe Johns at Carlsbad, New Mexico, and he was wanted for investigation of holdups in more towns than I would care to name. The time had passed when their friends and families could dismiss Bonnie and Clyde as a couple of good-time kids who had made some mistakes.

Little by little, law enforcement officers were learning more about Bonnie and Clyde from their old running mate Raymond Hamilton, who was cooling off in the Hillsboro jail at the end of 1932 and the beginning of 1933.

Hamilton said he parted company with Clyde, who was "too fast for me," not long after they escaped the ambush at Wharton. He admitted he had been in the car following Clyde and Bonnie when South Texas officers tried to catch them on a bridge over the Colorado. Hamilton would not tell much, but he enabled some more pieces of the Bonnie and Clyde story to be put together.

A spare boy of medium height and blond hair, Raymond and his older brother Floyd were two in a family of six children. The head of the house had deserted the family and left the children for the mother to raise. Ray had been born at Cedar Hill, a pleasant farm neighborhood then just to the south of Dallas, and, records show, his first arrest came at age fourteen. The boy stole a toy wagon.

Raymond didn't graduate into major crime until, in his new neighborhood in West Dallas as a teenager, he met Buck and Clyde Barrow. From them he learned that anyone could own a car for at least a few hours or a few days simply by getting into one and driving it away.

But while Clyde and Bonnie might have been satisfied to have only each other and enough money to get by on from small robberies and holdups, Hamilton got a taste of "big money" from two bank jobs accomplished with Clyde and Bonnie, and he liked it. He had a grandiose idea he could rise above the small holdups that were netting only small amounts and hit some of the larger banks.

When Raymond decided to go his own way for a holiday with his West Dallas pal Gene O'Dare, they went in style: this time, this one time, they bought Pullman tickets and made their way to Bay City, Michigan.

Hamilton's roving eye lingered there on a waitress. Basking too long in her attention, and with his good-sized roll of bills from recent robberies in Texas, young Hamilton couldn't resist laying on a story of how he was wanted in Texas for some crimes, including murder.

He couldn't have known that the waitress already had a man friend — who happened to be a policeman at Bay City.

Hamilton and his sidekick O'Dare were feeling good as they arranged a double date with the waitress and a friend to go skating. And, betrayed by their dates, they were captured easily in a place that allowed them no chance at all to resist or to flee — with skates on.

Brought back to Texas, they faced a series of charges that sent O'Dare back to prison immediately and sent Hamilton into a series of trials for his bank robberies, car thefts, and the shooting of J. N. Bucher in Hillsboro.

Hamilton wasn't the type of hoodlum who would languish behind bars without trying to get out. And what were friends for if they weren't to help Raymond Hamilton?

It was Ray's attempt to escape that brought me into the search for Bonnie and Clyde. On only the sixth day of Smoot Schmid's term as Dallas County sheriff — while my principal chore still was the delivery of subpoenas — Clyde Barrow and Bonnie Parker were to thrust themselves into my life and, in the course of a few hours, change my perspective on the deputy sheriff job I had reluctantly agreed to take.

Just before Smoot took office, during the Christmas holiday week of 1932, the Home Bank of Grapevine had been robbed of $2,800. Grapevine is just eighteen or twenty miles northwest of Dallas, and today it is booming, because that is where they've put the nation's largest airport, the Dallas-Fort Worth International Airport.

But in those days, Grapevine was remote and defenseless. It was just the size town with just the right size bank to have enough money to make it interesting for young bank robbers.

But local officials had some luck with that one; they captured one of the robber gang almost as soon as the robbery was finished. The suspect, named Les Stewart, balked for a time at telling the names of his accomplices. He was young and he was scared, but he insisted on keeping his secrets.

That was only a small inconvenience. Anyone with contacts in West Dallas, and I must confess I had my share, knew the people Les had been running with. Of course he knew Bonnie and Clyde — and the boy would be careful not to implicate them for reasons that surely would appear obvious. But he might implicate someone else who was in on the robbery. Finally he blurted out the name of Odell Chambless, a young man from a bootlegging family. To gain a possible favor with the officers, Chambless might ''get in touch'' with Clyde and Bonnie, Stewart thought, or with the family of Raymond Hamilton, who was in the Hillsboro jail at the moment.

It took no genius to conclude also that the gang might be using the home of one of Hamilton's two sisters, who lived in West Dallas, as a meeting place to plan capers or divide spoils of their crimes. One of Raymond's sisters was Mrs. Lillie McBride, whose house was at 507 County Avenue, not more than two blocks from the service station that Barrow's parents operated.

Fred Bradberry from the sheriff's office agreed to act on a tip that came from Dusty Rhodes and Walter Evans of the Tarrant County district attorney's office. They brought Tarrant County deputy Malcolm Davis and J. F. Van Noy, a special state Ranger from Belton. The tip was that they might learn something from Lillie McBride about the Grapevine Bank Robbery.

So often, tips pan out — but not quite the way they were received. And this was one example.

On Friday evening, January 6, 1933, when the officers arrived at the house to question Lillie, she wasn't at home. But an older sister, Mrs. Maggie Fairris was. Maggie was keeping her six-year-old daughter and also Lillie's seven-month-old son. Mrs. Fairris told the officers Lillie had "just stepped out to go to town and will be right back."

With their official cars out of sight, Rhodes, Bradberry and Van Noy settled in to chat with the young woman in the front room of the house for awhile. They waited longer; Lillie still had not returned. Mrs. Fairris put the children to bed. The young woman was acting strange, nervous, uneasy — but few women are accustomed to having three law enforcement officers drop in and remain. Tarrant deputy Malcom Davis and Walter Evans said they'd wait on the back porch, in the darkness.

Suddenly Bradberry said, "Douse the lights." Mrs. Fairris obliged — but she insisted that the six-year-old was accustomed to having the small red light on, so Bradberry agreed: "If the light is usually on at night, let it remain."

About midnight, Bradberry heard a car slow in front of the house, then heard it drive away. He cursed himself; the damned red light had tipped the whole trap. He put out the red light and remained at a position at the front window. Van Noy and Rhodes slipped into another room, to keep themselves hidden from the view of passersby. Davis and Evans still were waiting on the back porch.

Then, in only the time it would take for a car to have circled the block, Bonnie and Clyde and another man seated under the wheel pulled to a stop in front of the house. Clyde got out and started walking toward the house.

At that point, no one could be positive this was Barrow. It could easily have been anyone at all. Officers would have to use caution in any case.

"Go to the door, let him in," Bradberry whispered to Mrs. Fairris. "Do as I say."

Mrs. Fairris flung open the door and cried out excitedly — surely to warn Clyde that the house was full of officers. "Oh, no, don't shoot . . . think of my babies . . ."

Never one to be slow on the draw, or one to hesitate before firing, Clyde Barrow had all the warning he needed. He swiftly leveled his shotgun and fired through the front window at the point where surely he had seen the figure of Bradberry seated before the red light had been doused. Driven away from the window by the blast, Bradberry recovered in time to see Clyde backing away cautiously, his shotgun still drawn on the house.

Hearing the clatter of gunfire, Malcolm Davis ran from his post at the rear of the house, around the left side, and, seeing no one, turned to run into the house.

Another shotgun blast from Barrow filled Davis with buckshot. He crumpled face down on the porch into a pool of blood. Officers now were firing rapidly from the window, and pistol shots were answering from the car — Bonnie apparently firing to cover Clyde as he retreated to the car.

Officers fired twenty shots in the exchange, and Bonnie and Clyde together may have fired half that many. Even so, the pair with the mysterious "other man" had escaped another trap; they fled west on Eagle Ford Road, spitting gravel from their tires in their wake and receiving fire that hit the car but failed to stop them.

Bradberry and another officer tried to get Davis to Methodist Hospital, but he died before they arrived.

A call to the sheriff's office notified Schmid, and in only a few seconds Smoot called me personally to come down and get in on the investigation and the chase.

The next hours and days convinced me that there would be no way to remain out of the more lurid and active side of the sheriff deputy's office. Perhaps this is what I wanted all along and would not admit it. Smoot had sensed that, probably, and gradually worked on me with the idea that the process serving job would be something like the special delivery job I'd been holding with the post office.

By 3 A.M., Lillie McBride had returned to the house and was placed under arrest, and so was Lucile Hilburn, who was nineteen. Some shots in the exchange broke the windows of a house owned by W. B. Strait, fifty-nine, two doors away from the McBride house.

From Lillie we obtained information that Odell Chambless had called at her home and had stayed "not more than five minutes" to change his muddy army trousers and boots and lumberjack and put on some new clothes he had brought. But under questioning, she admitted Chambless had given her money, that she had gone into town and had bought him a complete set of clothes and had driven him to Tyler in a borrowed car.

While Lillie's statement definitely linked Chambless to the Grapevine Bank robbery, a carelessly made statement that she had been visiting her brother Raymond Hamilton at the Hillsboro jail caused some ears to perk up at the sheriff's department in Dallas.

A call to the jailer at Hillsboro confirmed where Lillie had been. "No, I didn't let her stay long; she just brought him that ol' radio . . . because he might be around awhile and wanted something to help him pass the time," the jailer drawled.

Radio! My God, that was how Hamilton had broken jail at McKinney when he first was picked up after the killing of Bucher. A radio smuggled into his cell had covered the noise of his sawing the jail bar.

A call to the sheriff at Hillsboro seemed to be the best prevention one could take. "If you'll go back to Hamilton's cell, I think you'll hear the radio playing — and you might catch Hamilton sawing his way out.''

The sheriff was grateful. Hamilton was in the act of doing just that. He was a hard man to hold.

We found out, a little later, that the reason for Clyde's visit to Lillie McBride's house on January 6 was just to be sure that Hamilton had received the radio. It figured in their plans to get back together and hit the road again.

VI

The Barrow Gang Forms

BUCK BARROW, Clyde's brother, served time at Huntsville but escaped by walking away from a prison work gang in 1930. Afterwards he married Blanche Caldwell, a fine girl whose law-abiding family owned a dairy farm. When Blanche discovered that Buck was, in fact, an escaped prisoner, her head was set:

Buck would turn himself in; he would serve out his sentence. Blanche promised she would wait as long as it took to "get right" by the law. And Buck must have believed her, for he drove with her to Huntsville Prison on December 27, two days after Christmas in 1931, and reminded prison officials he should be inside. Apparently he hadn't even been missed. He introduced his wife, Blanche, and his mother, Cumie, to prison officials and told the officials of his firm intention to complete his sentence and then rejoin his wife on the outside. "And never give anyone any more trouble," he promised.

Buck blamed himself for the fact that Clyde had gone into crime — and had graduated from the petty thievery that Buck had embraced to the most serious of crimes. In one of his prison jobs, when he was on a cleaning detail, he never could see the electric chair without a passing thought that his brother Clyde might be headed for it.

Blanche and Buck's mother succeeded in getting a pardon for Buck on March 22, 1933. But when he became a free man, and noticeably changed, he had a yearning to see his brother. The mere suggestion that he intended to ''go and see Clyde for awhile'' brought sadness to Blanche. She must have known, better than anyone, that Clyde could change Buck into a criminal again before Buck ever could convince Clyde to give up the fugitive life. And the whole family was aware that the time had long since passed that Clyde could expect anything but the electric chair if he was caught.

Apparently the Barrows were receiving letters regularly from Clyde — handwritten by Bonnie, signed by Clyde, and mailed from any place throughout the Southwest or Middle West that their travels might take them. The letters would say only that ''everyone is well'' and not much more. But the grapevine that Clyde and Bonnie had with their family — and so many West Dallas people were related in some way or other — always kept the family notified of their whereabouts.

Despite the protests of Blanche, and Buck's assurances that he ''wouldn't drive around the block with Clyde,'' the two went together to visit Clyde and Bonnie within a month after Buck's release from prison. The two couples and young W. D. Jones rented a stone bungalow in the Freeman Park Addition of Joplin, Missouri, with rooms above a double garage.

After a few days and nights of the reunion, which surely included the passing of tales of Buck's prison life and Clyde and Bonnie's escapades, neighbors began to notice some ''strange things'' about the new tenants. When the garage door opened, they noticed an unusual number of 1933 automobile license plates. They thought they saw an inordinate number of guns being carried into the car by two of the young men who lived in the quarters above.

The reports brought State Highway patrolmen G. B. Kahler and W. E. Grammer out to take a look. After three days of keeping a watch on the place, they brought three Joplin officers into the case. The strangers just might be the elusive Barrows, the officers reasoned.

Clyde and W. D. had gone out scouting for a place to stick up. By Jones's later account, the finances were down to eight dollars at one point. But after driving only a short distance, Clyde sensed that "something seemed funny" and they returned to the rented bungalow. Urgently, Clyde wheeled the car into the garage below the living quarters, locked the garage door, and ran upstairs with W. D.

Bonnie was cooking red beans and corn bread, and Blanche was playing solitaire. Buck was dozing on a couch. A dog was asleep nearby.

At that fateful moment, just at dusk on April 13, 1933, Constable J. W. Harryman slipped out of a Joplin police car and led officers toward the garage door. "Officers," Harryman called out.

Clyde and W. D. needed no reminder that "the law" had found them. Clyde called to Bonnie and to Buck and Blanche to "grab the guns." Only Blanche failed to respond quickly. Clyde and W. D. fired at the officers with powerful Browning Automatic Rifles from the garage door that they had opened slightly. Bonnie, standing in a negligee, fired from a window above them. The officers returned the fire in a few seconds. All hell had broken loose.

Constable Harryman, who got within ten feet of the garage, fell mortally wounded, without having a chance to hear any response other than the click of the weapon that fired the bullet that killed him. Detective Harry McGinnis ran toward the fallen officer, firing at the house as he approached. Officers heard Bonnie call out "Pour it on 'em, Clyde — we're coming down." Withering gunfire spitting from the powerful automatic rifles sent McGinnis scurrying for cover. He did not make it. He fell too, mortally wounded.

Trooper Kahler peppered the house with fire from behind a parked patrol car in the driveway, to cover Trooper Grammer's dash to find a telephone. Grammer was pleading desperately for reinforcements to help in the sickening fight when the fugitives found the moment right for their escape.

In the split seconds before reserves could reach them, and when two officers lay dying and two others were wounded, Clyde and W. D. were laying down a curtain of fire to discourage the remaining officers from firing on Bonnie. Bonnie had reached the car, loaded down with some of the guns and some of the ammunition. Blanche, her deck of cards frozen tightly in her hands, had hysterically run off, sobbing, down the street, the dog cradled in her arms. Clyde had caught a bullet in the shoulder; W. D. had a head wound that was spurting blood.

Buck kicked the garage door open from inside. Clyde, under cover of W. D.'s fire, had moved Constable Harryman's body that blocked the drive. As Clyde fired cover in turn for Jones, the young man raced to the police car that stood in the drive. He snatched open the door, released the brake, and gave the car a shove. Set rolling, the car zigzagged crazily into the street and settled on the opposite side. With the official car out of the way, Clyde leaped into the V-8 and shotgunned it out of the garage, with W. D. leaping on the running board as it turned into the street.

The wounded and dying officers could only fire at the departing car in a helpless gesture of the beaten. The Barrows — no mistaking them now — were making a getaway.

Two blocks away, the car screeched to a stop. Buck got out and pulled the whimpering and dazed Blanche into the car, still clutching her deck of cards, still cradling the dog in her arms. The car picked up speed and disappeared into the night. The "Barrow Gang" had chalked up another escape — and murders six and seven.

Word of the fight reached the sheriff's office in Dallas within a few minutes. Within an hour, Bob Alcorn called and said he had cleared it with Sheriff Schmid for me to accompany him to Joplin.

Newton County Constable J. W. Harryman apparently died as he lay in the driveway; Joplin Police Detective Harry McGinnis's arm was shot off, and he died a short time after the raid. Two other officers received lesser wounds.

As for the fugitives, officers knew only that Buck Barrow had been hit — though there was no way of knowing that the head wounds were as serious as they were. The wound suffered by W. D. Jones apparently was not serious at all. And Clyde apparently had been struck only by a bullet that had bounced off another surface. Sometime during the getaway ride, Bonnie actually removed it by digging at it with a hairpin, so near to the surface of Clyde's chest was it lodged.

Bob Alcorn and I drove through all of the night that remained and reached Joplin from Dallas the following morning — to be of any assistance we could in taking up the chase. But for the immediate time, two rolls of undeveloped film that had been among the many articles left behind had to be printed and then identified. We were needed for that chore.

In the apartment, along with the film and the mass of glass shards and unmade beds, Blanche's purse with her marriage license and Buck's pardon papers told us of their presence and something of the circumstance of their being where they were.

The film told us a great deal more — and may have set off more mistaken stories about the Barrows than anything that had turned up before or after that bloody and blazing night in Joplin. It was certain now, for the first time, that the mysterious young man frequently reported with them was W. D. Jones. This knowledge would free a former Barrow associate named Frank Hardy back in Texas; Hardy was, at that moment, accused of a crime that witnesses would come to believe Jones had committed instead.

The pictures showed a group having what they must have considered a delightful time. In one picture, Bonnie was pictured as she held a shotgun on Clyde. There were other poses of Buck and Blanche and W. D. Recognizable in one photograph — one that would make law enforcement officials more determined than ever to get the Barrows dead or alive — was the cockiness shown in photographs posing with the weapon taken from an officer who had been kidnapped and released by the fugitives.

And there was one that came to be circulated widely in the months and years ahead: the famous picture of Bonnie with a cigar in her mouth. Today, the mistake has been perpetuated into a cliche, that Bonnie was Clyde's ''cigar-smoking gun moll.'' Once a story like that has gained circulation over so many years, it is risky business attempting to set the record straight. But the fact is, Bonnie never smoked cigars; occasionally she smoked Lucky Strike cigarettes, but rarely. And in the original photograph, Bonnie held a rose in her mouth by the stem, not a cigar. The cigar was a Joplin newspaperman's little

Clyde, Bonnie, and W. D. Jones took the snapshots on the following pages in 1933. Clyde was 24, Bonnie 23, and W. D. 17.

CLYDE (LEFT) AND W. D. TOOK PRIDE IN DRESSING LIKE MEN OF THE
WORLD.

BONNIE AND W. D. JONES

W. D. Jones

CLYDE BARROW—HIS CAR WAS HOME.

CLYDE IN A PICTURE THAT WAS USED LATER FOR HIS "WANTED" POSTER.

BONNIE, LESS GUARDED THAN SHE APPEARS TO BE ON PAGE 42.

joke at the time. With some simple retouching, the rose became a cigar. That was something that could illustrate much better than any rose just what a tough young ninety-five-pound girl Bonnie Parker really was.

Nothing the newspapers or the crime magazines wrote about Bonnie ever annoyed her so much as the reference that she smoked cigars. But the power of suggestion and the impact of repetition is strong. In subsequent reports of supposed on-the-scene inspection of the Barrow hideouts, colorful newspaper reporters more than once found a way to say that "a big black cigar butt" was found. And one report even added that the cigar butt bore "Bonnie's tiny toothprints."

When we did not immediately pick up the trail of Clyde and Bonnie after we had helped the Missouri officers with the picture identification, and after we had exchanged information, Sheriff Schmid called us back to Dallas. Bonnie and Clyde, he said, would return to Dallas sometime; our chances for picking up their trail would be better if we left Missouri to the officers there. Alcorn protested, but Schmid had made his decision.

The next word we received that the gang was doing business as usual came about two weeks later. On April 28, Clyde and W. D. were cruising on North Trenton Street in Ruston, Louisiana, when the car slowed and W. D. quickly slipped into a car parked outside L. K. Brooks's boarding house. A pretty young lady named Sophie Stone was sitting on a porch swing, and a young man named H. D. Darby was inside the house having his lunch.

Darby was shocked when Miss Stone called excitedly that someone was driving his car away. Her own car was available and she suggested pursuing the thief if Darby wished. They'd read in the local paper of another bold car theft in their small town, and Darby was incensed.

They took up the chase. But, according to Clyde's sister, who later told the story as she heard it from Clyde, he was not seriously worried that anyone could overtake W. D. After all, he had taught W. D. a lot of things, and one was how to jump into a car, start it, and drive like a madman. Clyde was amused as he followed the pursuing car all the way to the town of Hilly, eighteen miles northwest of Ruston.

By that time Darby decided to give up the chase. He had to return to his job at a funeral parlor. And Miss Stone, who valued her job as the county home demonstration agent, felt she should return to work too. They turned Miss Stone's car around, and Darby believed he never would see his own car again.

But Clyde and Bonnie, and Buck and Blanche too, agreed to a little amusement. They overtook W. D. and suggested that he should turn around. Together now, in only the one car they had before the theft, they chased their pursuers back to Ruston. In a moment that was full of fun for the gang, and terror for Miss Stone and Darby, Clyde pulled up alongside and ordered them over.

Darby was sputtering. He recognized W. D. as the young man who had stolen his car, and where was it now? Too late the astonished couple recognized the Barrows, who were forcing them into their car.

By Miss Stone's account of the incident later, Clyde asked Darby why he would do such a foolish thing as to think he could overtake W. D., and why didn't the two of them just settle back and enjoy a ride until their captors decided what to do with them — perhaps to take them somewhere, tie them to a tree, and shoot them.

"They drove us around, endlessly it seemed, up in to Arkansas. They made jokes among themselves, and sometimes they were friendly and sometimes they made threats. But we were plain scared. By 2 A. M., after all those hours of riding in terror, we had become resigned that we would be killed. We had become so tired, Mr. Darby and I, that we didn't care if they killed us or not."

Once during the drive, Clyde became interested in talking.

"Clyde asked me what I did," Miss Stone related later. "I told him I was a home demonstration agent. Mr. Darby told him he worked in a funeral parlor. And Bonnie laughed at that and said 'When we get ours, you can fix us up real pretty.'

"At the end of the ride, when the Barrows had finished with their fun, they let us out just outside of Waldo, Arkansas. But instead of shooting us, they gave us five dollars so we could walk into Waldo and get a bus to take us back to Ruston.''

W. D. became separated from Clyde and Bonnie during the first week in June. As had happened before and would happen again with the bandit gang, a robbery would sometimes go awry, and the car would take off without one or other member getting picked up in the haste to make a getaway. In such a case, escape would be made separately by whatever means came handy and they could get back together later.

In early June, 1933, such a circumstance brought W. D. back to Dallas — and this brought my first encounter as a deputy sheriff with Clyde and Bonnie, when they came to reestablish contact with him.

I had no prior knowledge they were coming. No one in the sheriff's department had. It had become my personal practice at that time never to go running to the newspapers with information, as too many peace officers in that day were inclined to do. More than anyone would suspect, law breakers depended on newspaper accounts to supply them with information on what the law enforcement people were doing, how many officers were on the chase, where roadblocks were set up, and all that. We had no such advantage, and most of West Dallas was against us.

But the veteran deputy Bob Alcorn had taken a liking to me. He knew I'd stand my ground, knew I could shoot with anybody. And, with all modesty, I probably knew more people — particularly the hoodlums who were up to no good — than any other deputy on the force.

On several cases, it was helpful to know who was kin to whom, who was going around with whom, and most of all the relationships and allegiances that bonded people together. If there was any way of ''getting ahead'' in the sheriff's department, it had to be through the criminal division rather than the civil division, which had more people. At least the criminal division was where the action was — though not too many deputies saw much future in chasing Clyde Barrow.

As long as Clyde and Bonnie, and now Buck and W. D., were together and on the loose, there was no harm in keeping an eye out for them any time I wasn't busy with something else the sheriff assigned me to do. Even though, officially, that still wasn't my job. I certainly could see that Schmid was daily getting more pressure in the newspapers and around town to bring in Clyde and Bonnie. The work he had already done in getting the business affairs of the department straightened up brought him some good will for a few months. But here it was June, and the clamor was growing to get the Barrows.

In my Ford V-8 roadster, alone or with any officer who would accompany me, I was beginning to spend more and more of my nights just driving around or keeping a lookout on the off chance I might hear something or see them. It was on one such occasion, on June 19, 1933, I first met them as a deputy. I was in my roadster; I spotted someone who looked like Clyde — who *was* Clyde. I gave chase. The encounter amounted to no more than that. I had missed them, had been outrun. By the time I could get word back to the sheriff's department there was no way we could catch them ourselves. We alerted some other officers in other cities by telephone. The only real piece of information I had was that they weren't with Buck and Blanche when they were in Dallas that night.

In the light of accounts that came much later, the reason Clyde and Bonnie were in Dallas became clear enough: W. D. had passed the word to a member of the family where he would be when Clyde and Bonnie returned for him. By their prearrangement, it was all accomplished. I had recognized them and given a chase in which I was badly outclassed in the car I was driving.

Within weeks I saw them again and was outrun again. The trail that brought Clyde back to Dallas this time began on June 10. That day he and Bonnie and W. D., together again, were speeding along a road seven miles west of Wellington, in Collingsworth County up in the Texas Panhandle not far from the Oklahoma line, to a rendezvous with Buck, who was at a prearranged spot near Erick, Oklahoma. Abruptly, the car hurtled over an embankment where a bridge was out. No barricades were left to warn them. Miraculously, considering the way Clyde always drove, they weren't killed outright. The car must have rolled and overturned before coming to a jolting stop in the shallow canyon. Jones was dazed, but Clyde managed to free himself and help W. D. out. But Bonnie was pinned inside, and now the car started to burn. Clyde screamed for help that already was on the way through the darkness.

Two farmers named Pritchard and Carter appeared like Samaritans to help. As Clyde was frantically trying to console Bonnie, who was painfully and seriously burned despite W. D.'s efforts to throw sand on the flames to extinguish them, the farmers threw their shoulders onto the car and, with Clyde and W. D. helping, managed to remove Bonnie tenderly and carry her to the farmhouse nearby. The farm wife of Pritchard hurriedly prepared fresh sheets for a bed and led the menfolk carrying the tiny Bonnie to it. By the light of a kerosene lamp, Mrs. Pritchard dressed the burns on Bonnie's arms, face, chest, and legs with a vinegar bath and wet soda, a home remedy for burns on a farm at that time.

"She needs burn salve," said the farm woman. "What she really needs is a doctor."

Clyde had managed to slip back to the burning car and remove the guns. When he returned to the house and found W. D. waiting idly on the porch, he was distressed to find that one of the farmers had disappeared.

"Where's the other guy?" Clyde asked Pritchard, who was busy "getting things" for his wife to help with the nursing of Bonnie inside.

"He's gone to call a doctor," Pritchard told him.

Carter hadn't really gone to call a doctor. He had slipped away, and then run in a lope, to a telephone that would notify the local sheriff. Carter had caught sight of the guns in the car; he had read the newspaper stories and heard on the radio of a half dozen criminals that were in the news at that time, from Pretty Boy Floyd and Woodrow Underhill to Bonnie and Clyde and another fellow. "May not be anything," he had cautiously told Sheriff George T. Corry on the telephone, "but I'd sure appreciate it if you'd come out and take a look out by that old bridge that's out."

W. D. was annoyed at himself that he had allowed Carter to leave; his head still was reeling, and he disliked as much as anything that Clyde was sore at him. He knew Clyde was mad by the way Barrow thrust a shotgun in his hand as he appeared from the burning car, gruff-like, and then walked in to be with Bonnie.

With the shotgun, W. D. began to badger the Pritchards, to tell them they'd better not try anything funny. "We weren't doing anything but trying to help," Pritchard said, wishing that the sheriff would appear. "The girl is going to have to have a doctor or she's not going to make it," Mrs. Pritchard declared.

Clyde was distraught. Out of his mind distraught. At Bonnie's side one minute and agonizing over his plight the next, walking to the porch, staring out into the night western sky, seeing the glow from the fire that was consuming the car in a gulley where the bridge was out.

Then a shot rang out. Knowing that the call Carter had planned to make was not for a doctor but for the sheriff, Mrs. Pritchard bolted out of the back door on a run. W. D., not knowing what to do, called out to her, "Don't leave!" and fired. A shotgun blast left the woman's hand torn and dangling like strands spurting blood. Her husband, mad as hell but silent, ran to her with towels to staunch the flow of blood.

Finally he said, "Is this the way you repay kindness?" Jones could do nothing now except hold the gun on the couple who had befriended them. Bonnie suddenly bolted upright and made ready to run. Clyde and W. D. saw a car approach; they slipped out of the house, out of view of Sheriff Corry and Wellington Town Marshal Tom Hardy.

Just as the officers approached the back step of the house, Clyde and W. D. had the drop on them. The young fugitives jolted them from behind, took their weapons, and clamped their wrists with their own handcuffs.

Corry and Hardy would be added to the list of Barrow kidnap victims. They were forced into the sedan they arrived in. Clyde returned to the house to help Bonnie to the car, placed her beside Hardy in the back seat. With Corry sandwiched between Clyde and Jones, Clyde wheeled the car back to the road and sped hell bent on a three-hour ride to a place on a lonely road outside Erick, Oklahoma.

Apparently the spot had been predetermined. Clyde rolled the car to a stop. W. D. went straightaway to a rusty barbed-wire fence alongside the road, ripped some of the wire apart, and Clyde led the officers to a nearby tree. With the wire, they secured the handcuffs together and tied the officers to the tree. Buck Barrow and Blanche appeared while this indignity was being performed. And while Blanche took up the care of Bonnie's burns, which obviously were a surprise to her, Buck asked if Clyde was planning to shoot the officers.

Clyde said he decided not to do it. Grinning through the grease on his face that bore blisters from the fire, Clyde explained, "I'm beginning to like them. They were real nice to Bonnie."

Bonnie was carried to Buck's car. The officers glumly watched their kidnappers drive away. It was thirty minutes before they could free themselves by continually moving and bending the rusted wire that had bound them. In those thirty minutes, with Clyde at the wheel, the fugitives were forty miles from Erick. And they did not stop, except to fill their gas tank, until they had crossed Oklahoma west to east and reached the outskirts of Fort Smith, Arkansas.

Bonnie's condition apparently was far worse than Clyde had supposed. At Fort Smith — throwing away his usual caution — he rented a double tourist court cabin and boldly asked the manager to call a doctor. The burns, he explained, were caused when their kerosene camp stove exploded.

The doctor who attended Bonnie apparently had not been reading the newspapers. Either that, or, as one might suppose, he was told that he could be found and shot if he related anything of what he was doing or seeing. He treated the burns, suggesting hospitalization for Bonnie. If that couldn't be arranged, the very least he should recommend, he said, was that a nurse be hired for around-the-clock care.

Apparently, too, Bonnie became delirious. Her frequent cries for her mother on Sunday, June 19 — nine days after the incident at Wellington — brought Clyde to the verge of capture. It was at noon that day that Clyde drove alone to Dallas. He made straight for Mrs. Parker's house and brought the news of Bonnie's condition. Both Clyde's mother and Mrs. Parker pleaded to be allowed to return with him to Bonnie. Clyde wouldn't permit that, but he thought the presence of

Bonnie's sister, Billie, might be a consolation to her. And Billie's absence from Dallas would not arouse police suspicion nearly so much as a sudden vacation by either of the mothers.

As a personal note, I am certain that I would have noticed if either of the two had remained away from their homes for more than a few days. I had, in fact, paid a call on both Mrs. Barrow and Mrs. Parker just a short time after the reports came from Wellington about Bonnie's burns and the subsequent kidnapping of the two officers. Her mother had noted a story in one of the papers, and had heard opinions of neighbors, that "Clyde will shoot Bonnie and leave her alongside some lonely road." The reasoning was that Clyde couldn't afford to risk taking her with him while she wasn't able to walk. I had told Mrs. Parker to forget it — it wouldn't happen that way. She wanted to believe that. There was no point at all in making her life worse than it was. God knows, the woman was going through the torment of hell without having that to worry her.

Events proved that the callous opinions about Clyde's loyalty — where Bonnie was concerned — were dead wrong. Clyde risked his life to drive to Bonnie's mother in Dallas. And that is when I had my second frustrating encounter with him. It was near midnight on Sunday, June 19, that I caught sight of a man who could only have been Clyde. I was determined to make certain — though I really couldn't have been more sure. I was confused because I did not recognize the young woman beside him as Bonnie. But for a fleeting second, my eyes met with Clyde's as his car came in the direction I had come from. I saw that he recognized me, saw his car dig in and speed faster. My heart pounded; I spun my roadster into a U-turn and held the pedal on the floorboard. In a moment, or perhaps even less, I had lost sight of him. I followed for a few lonely minutes more in the night, as fast as my car would go, perhaps eighty. But deep down I knew I was beaten again. I could only return to a telephone and report another sighting; I could hold some hope a roadblock could be thrown up somewhere and that Clyde and his companion, whom I did not recognize in the dark except to feel that she was not Bonnie, could be stopped some place down the line.

But it was futile to believe that.

This was an experience, however, that convinced me I wanted to get officially into the chase to run Clyde and Bonnie down. I would find a way to get a faster car. I would learn to use a weapon even better than I already knew. Then I would see if Sheriff Schmid would allow me to . . .

That's crazy, I would tell myself. Plain crazy. But I decided that at the very least I would have some work done on my car to give it more speed.

The record later would show that Bonnie's sister, Billie, returned with Clyde to the tourist cabin near Fort Smith before the sun rose that morning. Bonnie came out of her delirium and recognized her sister in the tourist cabin hideout three days later, when she began a tedious recovery that left her in a very sickly condition for weeks.

The frequent change of dressings required for the burns, the doctor bill, the tourist cabin rental, and the nursing care — plus whatever inducement may have been paid to assure that no word of their identity leaked out — left the funds depleted again.

Law enforcement officers who were trying to find them could only wait for the next word of a crime that appeared to be the work of the Barrows. Alcorn and I had talked about them on one of our rides around the city together. We expected to read of a sizeable amount of money in accounts of the very next daring robbery they tried. And it was no satisfaction at all that we were right.

With Billie present, along with Buck and Blanche, to tend Bonnie's burns, Clyde and W. D. could easily remedy their financial embarrassment.

At Alma, Arkansas, before noon on June 22, they forced the town marshal, Henry D. Humphrey, to accompany them to the Alma Bank. Using him as a hostage, and drawing their guns on the bank's few employees, they tied Humphrey to a pillar while employees, at their command, trundled the bank's safe to a truck waiting outside. The bank later reported its loss at three thousand dollars.

The next day they added a few hundred more with robberies of the two Piggly-Wiggly groceries at Fayetteville, Arkansas, and were seen leaving in Clyde's usual fashion — speeding hell-for-leather down U.S. 71 into the Boston Mountain country toward Alma, fifty miles distant, where they'd robbed the bank the day before.

As chance would have it, an acquaintance of the marshal spotted Humphrey, the officer who had been humiliated by the bank robbers, parked on U.S. 71. "What are you doing?" he called.

What was he doing? He had just received a telephone message from officers at Fayetteville that Clyde Barrow was headed back this way. This was an opportunity to redeem himself, redeem the humiliation of being led into a bank and tied up.

The town marshal's friend, a man named Wilson, was blocking the line of traffic, and speeding up behind him was a car that just might be the tan car Humphrey had been waiting for. He waved his friend to hurry on, and Wilson lurched forward. But the car behind was closing in, squealing its brakes, and the bumpers collided.

Wilson was mad as hell when he cut his ignition, opened his car door, grabbed a pair of good-sized rocks and straightened up, glaring at Clyde Barrow. He fully intended, it appeared, to give the careless fellows a bad time for crashing into the rear of his car. Then — recognizing the fugitives from pictures he had seen in the papers — Wilson dropped his rocks and ran.

There was no response coming from the car that had struck Wilson from behind. Perhaps they were seriously hurt. Humphrey decided to walk to the car, some fifty yards away, and have a look. His deputy, Salyers, walked behind Humphrey. The license number seemed to match the one he had heard broadcast, though he wasn't sure.

Salyers heard Humphrey call out, "Come out — and throw up your hands."

Clyde and W. D. opened the doors on opposite sides of the car and came out firing, using the open doors as shields. Humphrey fell dead, a hole in his chest. Now Salyers was alone to face the pair. He fired, and was fired upon. He ran; he darted, fired, and darted again, until his ammunition was gone and he had to reload. There was nothing to do but run now or die. He sought the safety of a nearby barn as a haven that would give him time to reload.

Rather than pursue him, the fugitive killers of Town Marshal Humphrey elected to make a run for Humphrey's car and escape in it.

As events would unfold, the car blew a tire a short time later — but a passing motorist was unfortunate enough to arrive and offer help. He was pulled from his car and left on the roadside as he watched Clyde and W. D. jump inside his car and drive away in it, heading into the mountainous area near Winslow, Arkansas.

This was termed good news when officers heard about it. Surely, this time the Barrows could be caught. That was the only road in and out of the area, a dead end. The word spread; a posse formed, and a plan to trap the sought-after pair was eagerly drawn.

Meanwhile, according to a later report by a woman named Mrs. Frank Rogers, two men tried to take her car but abandoned it after backing it into a tree almost as soon as they got it. And even as the posse was forming, the fugitives apparently returned to the highway, making their way on foot until they found a farmer carrying his produce to market. They simply hitched a ride, passing all the excitement as they rode on a vegetable truck to Fort Smith.

Clyde and W. D. found a telephone there; there is no other way to explain how Buck managed to find a car and get the women to a mountain hideout where they would be rejoined by the boys, who were out making their forays to get the money for Bonnie's treatments.

They couldn't have remained long in the hills. Later reports would show that Billie returned alone to Dallas on a train from Sherman on Sunday night, June 26. A short time afterward, a doctor in Enid — in the north central part of Oklahoma — reported a car stolen with his doctor's black bag in it. A National Guard armory in that same small city reported theft of a veritable arsenal of military weapons, notably the deadly Browning Automatic Rifles and ammunition enough for a regiment of marines in combat.

But while the search moved to the Enid area, apparently Clyde and Blanche were attending Bonnie at a hideout in Great Bend, Kansas. And though finances apparently were no serious problem for the moment, W. D. and Buck were making small robberies in Iowa and Illinois, confusing the law enforcement officers or anyone desiring to pick up the trail of Clyde and Bonnie.

For nearly three weeks, Bonnie could recuperate without interruption. In Dallas, we were waiting and watching and wondering where they were. No one hereabouts had heard a word. That was the story we were getting.

It was inevitable that the quiet could not last.

VII

Hell Breaks Out in Platte City

THE ENTIRE Southwest was feeling an edginess. Shop-keepers in obscure towns throughout Texas, Oklahoma, Louisiana, and Missouri seldom passed a day without some dread that the Barrow Gang would appear. Those were strange times. But in West Dallas, on my regular rounds, I frequently went out to pass cordial greetings with Clyde's father, Henry Barrow, and his mother, Cumie. I was keeping an eye on their place, of course, in the event that I could learn something that would help our department. But I believe, too, that I felt a deep sympathy for Henry and Cumie.

Mrs. Barrow, in July, expressed her own feelings openly to me. Her two sons, along with Bonnie and Blanche, were "all living on borrowed time." And she was sorrowful that she was powerless to do anything to stop the course of what was happening now and what surely would happen sooner or later to them. There was no way that she would turn them over to law enforcement officers — though I know she wished they could somehow turn themselves in with some guarantee of immunity from the electric chair. Prison, after all, would be a place of safety for them, compared to what they were undergoing.

"The troubles I've seen!" she said once. "Little Marvin is ten now, Mr. Hinton — and that boy hasn't even seen his

Daddy in six years," she said in the depth of her sadness. Marvin was Buck's son by a marriage previous to his present one with Blanche. There'd be no sons or daughters to carry on from Clyde and Bonnie's relationship, because Bonnie had had some trouble trying to have a child with Roy Thornton when she was too young. After the doctor had performed his surgery, Bonnie lost any hope for a child of her own.

But even as I was speaking on a regular basis to the Barrow parents, the feeling about their progeny everywhere else in the Southwest was only one of terror. Any rumor about them would spread quickly — and the rumor generally made them sound even more ruthless than they were. One rumor that persisted for a few anxious days in the summer of 1933 was that Clyde and Buck were together again and were planning a dramatic break-in of the federal prison at Leavenworth, Kansas, to free a third brother.

The rumor gained some credence with the discovery that there was, in fact, a man named Barrow in the prison. But he was unknown to the Barrows of West Dallas, and certainly not a relative. But when Clyde and Buck were identified with the theft of military weapons from the National Guard Armory at Enid, Oklahoma, there was more fuel for the scary rumors. At one time the number of lawmen and armor moving into the Cookson Hills of eastern Oklahoma bore a similarity to a major military movement. The reaction to a report that the Barrows were somewhere in the mountainous and inaccessible hills was quick and sure.

But overnight, on July 18, 1933, the search was abandoned in Oklahoma and taken up in a region around Fort Dodge, Iowa. In rapid succession, a Ford sedan with three men and two women (that would be Clyde and Buck Barrow, W. D. Jones, and Bonnie and Blanche) robbed three filling stations in Fort Dodge. All three victims were positive in their identification of photographs of all but the mysterious younger man who turned out to be Jones, and the "other" woman, who was the frightened Blanche. And all witnesses had noticed bandages on the arms of Bonnie Parker.

In the amount of cash lost, the robberies had not amounted to much. But the frustration felt by Iowa officers was a feeling that I would come to know in the months ahead. Just when it appeared that the bandits had sped away, a farmer also came in to have a look at the pictures. He had, he said, seen a group of people camp on his farm just a while before the robberies. He had paid little attention to them, for in those Depression years many people were "on the road," too poor to pay room rent in a tourist cabin as they shifted about the country.

But the farmer said he examined the site where they had been and he found discarded bandages. He had read in the newspapers about the bandit gang from Texas and about the woman who had been badly burned. He thought it was his duty to report what he had seen.

The alert went out immediately. But shortly after 10 P. M. that same July 18, the Ford sedan bearing the Barrows drove to the Red Crown Cabin Camp at the junction of U.S. 71 and Missouri State Highway 59, six miles southeast of Platte City.

Attendant Delbert Crabtree recalled later that it was a slight and pretty woman with reddish hair who rented the cabins and paid in advance, mostly with small change. And, yes, he seemed to remember one of the women had bandages on her arms, though he wasn't precisely sure. Two men and one woman were in the cabin on the left side of the two single garages that divided the cabins rented by the travelers. And a man and woman occupied the cabin on the right. Once he turned over the keys to the customer, they opened the garage door on one side; they drove the car in, and closed the door after it. A short time later, the red-haired young woman came into the filling station office and store to buy five sandwiches and beer.

After that, Crabtree told officers sometime later, he hardly gave them a thought. At mid-morning the following day, the redhead came in to pay for another night's use of the cabins and bought five large chicken dinners and soft drinks. The bill for the chicken dinners and drinks came to ten dollars. And, again, it was paid in quarters, dimes, and nickels.

Though Crabtree had really seen only the red-haired Blanche, he had read about the Barrows and had seen in the papers that there were five members of the fugitive gang. He thought he should relate this coincidence to his employer, M. D. Houser, who felt he should call it to the attention of Captain William Baxter of the Kansas City area office of the Missouri Highway Patrol.

Baxter drove down in the early evening to confer with Platte County Sheriff Holt Coffey.

At the Red Crown Tourist Cabins, Clyde was concerned that Bonnie's burn ointment had run out. He would go into Platte City and get more at a drugstore before it closed. But, cautious about leaving the rest of the group without a car, Clyde decided he would hitchhike in from the place known locally as "the Junction." What he found was a town already abuzz with the rumor that the notorious Barrow Gang was hereabouts.

Sheriff Coffey and Captain Baxter of the Platte City police department agreed to conduct a raid jointly. Coffey called in Deputies George Borden and Lincoln Baker, and Deputy Constables Byron Fisher and Thomas Hullett. Captain Baxter brought in Sergeant Thomas Whitecotton and Patrolman L. A. Ellis from the Platte City police department. And Sheriff Coffey permitted his son, Clarence, who was nineteen, to join the raiding party.

But an act of caution delayed the raid. The Barrow Gang's reputation was awesome. Instead of charging immediately into the suspected hideout, Captain Baxter convinced Sheriff Coffey that the raid could be more effective simply by surrounding the cabins and waiting for the fugitives to emerge.

At that moment in a downtown drugstore, D. R. Clevenger, the Platte County prosecutor, chanced to walk in. A clock on the wall showed 8 P. M., and, at this time of summer, darkness had only now begun to settle over the town. An acquaintance recognized the prosecutor and called out, "What's going on out at the Junction? I noticed all the police."

Clyde, unnoticed except as a customer wearing a blue shirt that was open at the collar, paid for his purchases and left the store. Clevenger was not curious at the moment about the stranger. But he went to a telephone and called the Houser station at the Red Crown Cabins six miles distant at the Junction for Sheriff Coffey, to find out why the police were there. In a moment Coffey came on the line. "I can't talk over the phone — just come on out," were Coffey's instructions.

Clevenger sped to the Junction and agreed that a raid could be justified. But he reconsidered. "Why not call the sheriff in Kansas City, bring out an armored car with steel shields for the men, and machine guns to rake the cabins?"

It was agreed. These may have appeared to be extreme measures to take — but the desire to take Clyde and Bonnie was extreme. They would wait about ninety minutes more for the armored car, the steel shields, and machine guns.

At 9 P. M., the officers saw the lights go out in the cabins both to the right and left of the twin garage doors that separated the reddish-brown brick cabins. Sometime after that hour, unseen by the officers who had surrounded the cabins, Clyde Barrow must have made his way back in the darkness to the cabins with the medicine obtained in Platte City. Later, none of the officers remembered seeing anyone enter the cabin from the outside.

Now, with the Jackson County officers providing reinforcement with the additional firepower and armored car, the attack plan became operational. Deputy George Highfill was instructed to move the armored car into place in front of the garage door to block any possible exit by the car that was inside the garage. On signal, Sheriff Coffey would identify himself and order the fugitives to come out. Deputy Thorpe, from inside the armored car, would bathe the cabin with the spotlight's glare.

The rest of the officers formed a veritable ring around the cabin, as Coffey advanced behind a steel shield:

"Officers! Come out!" he commanded.

The answering voice of a woman (it was Blanche) said, "Just a minute. Let me get dressed." Then, after a few seconds, the same voice called out, "They're in the other cabin!" Inside the cabin, unknown to the officers, all five of the fugitives now were awake. Clyde, waiting for darkness, had probably just returned; Bonnie was asleep, and Buck (according to Blanche's later recollection) was snoring softly. Clyde leaped up at the first noise and opened the cabin door into the closed garage, throwing some weapons inside the car.

But officers still were trusting the woman's voice — that she would momentarily be dressed and would greet them. They were cautious in the event that the people inside were not the Barrows at all. But suddenly this doubt was removed.

The cracking staccato of deadly Browning Automatic Rifle fire raked the police car and rained onto the armored vehicle.

Now the machine guns of the officers were answering; bullets tore through the garage doors. Glass from windows shattered. The officers were exposed in their positions by the very light that spotlighted the cabins. And worse, the armored car itself was taking fire; the bullets of the military B.A.R's were coming through it as if it were cardboard.

As bullets ricocheted off the brick walls or made splinters of the garage doors, Deputy Highfill inside the armored car cringed in pain. The withering fire had pierced the armor and Highfill discovered he had been hit through both knees. Thorpe continued to rake his machine gun fire across the white fronts of the twin garages, on the off chance this would slow the hail of bullets raining from it. Then in a rotten piece of luck, the machine gun in the armored car refused to fire. A chip of glass from the shattered overhead window had fallen into the mechanism.

From inside, W. D. momentarily was firing cover for Clyde as he hurriedly lifted Bonnie through the cabin door to the closed garage and into the car. Buck was holding a mattress as a kind of shield as Blanche, too, slid into the back seat of the car.

Outside, Sheriff Coffey raised his head to get a better look from behind his protective sheet of steel armor. "Get down, Dad," his son called out, and lurched toward the sheriff. A bullet struck Sheriff Coffey in the neck, and he was jerked to the ground by the impact. The boy, too, was hit. He was sent smashing to the ground with a bullet wound in his arm and another piece of metal tearing into his cheek.

Deputy Highfill, in tremendous pain inside the armored car and with his machine gun inoperative, told Thorpe to leave him to his fate with the car and "make a run for it."

Thorpe suggested something else: "Let's back the car out; you handle the wheel and I'll shift the gears."

The decision played into the hands of the trapped fugitives. For in the instant that the armored car moved away from the garage door it had been blocking, Clyde, W. D., and Buck were ready to pour it on.

As the armored car began backing away, a chance shot from the ringing and clattering fire coming from the cabins short-circuited its horn. The honking did not stop. Other officers reacted to the horn, believing it might be a signal to hold their fire. They ran toward the armored car and took up positions behind it.

Unknown to the officers, Buck Barrow had been hit twice in the head. Sobbing, desperate, and hysterical in the darkness inside their car, Blanche shrieked in a silent second amid the battering gunfire: "He's dying . . . dying . . ." But in a second, with W. D. on the running board, the Barrow car would come screaming out of the garage like a shot while W. D. held on precariously, raking the area with covering fire.

There was no accounting for it, no way to explain it. But the Barrow Gang, badly bloodied, was escaping a trap once more. Fire from the officers laced the departing car, shattering its glass, flattening its two rear tires. Blanche believed she was blinded as blood filled her eyes, though her wounds proved to be superficial. Buck's head wounds were severe, though the fugitives may not have realized that at the time. In any case, they chose not to give themselves up to have him attended in surgery.

The youth, Clarence Coffey, was rushed to Bethany Hospital in Kansas City, Kansas; Deputy Highfill was patched up at St. Joseph's in Kansas City. Sheriff Coffey ignored his wounds as a man fired by the excitement of the chase sometimes can. He posted guards at the cabins to assure that nothing would be disturbed until daylight.

And then he began regrouping his posse to pick up the trail of the fugitives.

BONNIE AND CLYDE

VIII

A Twenty-Acre Battleground

THERE WAS little consolation in the knowledge that the Barrow Gang had been bloodied in the fight at Platte City. So far as the officers involved in the scrap were concerned, the defeat — again — had been complete. The second-guessing started immediately: why had the armored car been removed from its blocking position in front of the garage door? How could so many officers have allowed five people — three of them either disabled or, in the case of Blanche, too hysterical to think of firing a weapon — to escape such a trap? The officers could not understand it themselves.

The awful fact was that the legend of Clyde and Bonnie would grow. They would kill again. And again.

The morning brought a report that warmed up the cold trail of the fugitives. A farmer named Cleve Burrell, who lived four miles east of Platte City, reported he had been awakened some time after midnight by two men and two young women. They wanted to borrow a motor car jack. When Burrell went to get the jack, the callers disappeared, so he returned to bed. But a short time later he was awakened again by the same four people. They accepted the use of his jack; they changed a wheel on their car and left the old wheel beside the road.

Coffey's men determined the wheel matched those on the getaway car.

But Burrell was certain he had seen only two men and two women: what had happened to the third man? Had Buck Barrow's wounds been more serious than officers had supposed? Could he have died and, if so, would the gang have buried him along some lonely road nearby?

A search of the area around the Burrell farm turned up more clues about the gang members and the extent of their wounds. A bloodied dress, so stained that the original color could not be determined, had been discarded. Ugly clumps of blood were on newspapers that apparently had been spread for a wounded man to lie on. There were other articles, including blood-soaked bandages. Coffey's men were certain now that more than one of the fugitives had been hit.

It is possible, from information that came to me later, to fill in portions of the story that were impossible for officers to know at the time. One is the fact that Buck had been shot twice in the head; one of the bullets had entered at one temple and had emerged at the other. His young wife, Blanche, had not made much of her own wound that seriously threatened the sight of one of her eyes when glass showered on her as bullets raked the bandit car in the getaway. Bonnie's burns were some time healing; she still required help in moving about.

During the flight, often without lights as the bullet-torn car rattled over backcountry roads, Blanche pleaded that Buck was in a bad fix; he needed hospital treatment even if it meant turning themselves in.

But even in a semiconscious condition and delirious, Buck sided with Clyde: only the electric chair awaited them now if they were caught. They would keep on driving. The pain and suffering in that car surely must have been intense, and this could only have been heightened by the out-of-the-head ravings of the wounded.

After the incident at the Burrell farm, where they changed the wheel on the car — probably while Buck remained out of sight at the place where the newspapers and other effects were found — they took up their drive again until they had crossed into Iowa. At Mount Ayr, indications were found sometime later that they had stopped at a stream for scrubbing up, and apparently they also burned some discarded bandages.

By late afternoon, human endurance must have faded, and the weary group found a likely place to stop at Dexfield Park, a grassy area of green, dotted with trees and surrounded by a veritable forest with covering underbrush that led down to a river. The park must have been a comforting sight for them. It offered a place to lay Buck down, a place where Blanche could sit at his side as he slipped in and out of consciousness. And though they couldn't have known it at the time, almost nobody in that area of hard-working farmers ever came to the recreational park and picnic spot except on weekends.

After two days, Buck was showing no signs of improvement. Bonnie still was a near invalid. Blanche's eye was worsening behind her dark glasses that hid the wound from Buck.

Clyde and W. D. decided they would have to have two cars if they were to continue; they drove into town for medical supplies first — alcohol to sterilize Buck's wounds, bandages and salve for Bonnie and Blanche. And a hypodermic to ease Buck's pain. And, of course, food. No one had eaten for two days. They returned to the hiding place in the park with all they went after, including five chicken dinners in paper bags. And no one seemed to recognize them.

Clyde and W. D. went to Perry and stole Edward Stoner's sedan. It was easy. W. D. drove the newly acquired sedan and Clyde followed back to the park.

The investigation and search still centered in Platte City and Joplin, where the Barrows recently had been. The FBI was in the case, primarily because the Barrows were principal suspects in the theft of government weapons from the Enid Armory. Hospitals in three or four states were alerted to report to authorities and detain any gunshot victims who came in for treatment.

Descriptions of the fugitives were pouring out of every radio, but the hunted gang was not listening to radio. A motorist who had come upon their parked car at Mount Ayr, on the Iowa side of the Missouri line, remembered that he had seen a badly wounded man lying on the back seat of a car that fit the description of the Barrow car he had heard about. He remembered that two other men and two women were burning something over a small campfire near the road. When he stopped to inquire, they all scrambled into their car and drove away in haste.

But a search of the area around Mount Ayr turned up nothing except the partially burned bandages and no other sign of the Barrows' presence. Obviously not. They were nestled in a secluded park between Dexter and Redding, Iowa.

With two cars, the fugitives now could take a ride together to break the monotony and perhaps to find another place to recover without pressing their luck too long at their hideaway.

Certainly there was no opportunity for us to know at that time how near the Barrow Gang may have been to giving themselves up. But at one time, apparently even Clyde had decided he should keep a promise made to his mother — that if either of them, he or Buck — or Bonnie — was seriously hurt, one would return the other to her in West Dallas so he would be with her. At one time Clyde even came to the point of saying, ''We're going back,'' and he had Blanche's vote on this; Buck was too near death to make a decision. But events prevented that from happening:

A farmer named Henry Penn was taking a stroll through Dexfield Park on Sunday afternoon, July 23, 1933. The fugitives had been driving around the area, scouting the territory and learning the roads. A spent campfire caught Penn's attention. Partially burned bloody bandages and a floormat that someone had tried to burn were unusual enough to report to the sheriff. Penn had heard things on the radio about some desperadoes from Texas. He said he couldn't see any harm in keeping an eye on the place.

Penn's call to Sheriff C. A. Knee and Special Deputy John Love of the Vigilantes of Dallas County, Iowa, set in motion one of the largest traps ever laid for fugitives. The officers began to rally all the heavily armed men they could place around the resort park, while Penn kept watch with one of the deputies from a secluded clump of shrubbery.

As lawmen were being notified, and while they headed to Dexfield Park from many points, the Barrow Gang returned in two cars to the campsite in the late afternoon. Darkness came, the campfire was lighted, and still there was no move on the lawmen's part to move in. They intended to surround the camp quietly during the night, notify the Iowa National Guard, the Des Moines Police, and the Iowa State Board of Investigation. Further, they would welcome any farmers with rabbit guns. Sheriff Knee did not intend to underestimate the cunning of the Barrows this time.

Despite the assembly during the night of upwards of forty armed men encircling the twenty-acre park itself, and perhaps twice that many detailed to block all roads leading away from the area, the movement was carried out without noise that would eliminate the surprise planned shortly after dawn. There were riot guns, machine guns, shotguns, and .22 rifles; the National Guardsmen had their standard government weapons. There were tear gas bombs, too.

Clyde and W. D. apparently spent most of the night tuning the motors of the cars by the soft and pencil-thin glare of a flashlight. Surely, the fugitives were bone weary; this may account for the fact that the twenty-acre forested and rolling plot could be ringed with armed men during the night without the Barrows being aware of any movement at all.

Daylight came and the camp began to stir. W. D. was roasting wieners; Blanche was frying eggs bought during their Sunday afternoon drive. Bonnie was making coffee. Clyde had lighted a cigarette for Buck and was smoking one himself — a rare thing for Clyde to do. This morning, as the sun rose over Dexfield Park, Clyde was talking again seriously of getting Buck back to Dallas.

Softly but firmly, Sheriff Knee ordered, "Let's close it up — and be careful." The deadly business was ready to begin. The manhunters began, as quietly as they could, to advance on the camp, moving from behind one tree to one nearer.

Suddenly, a twig snapped. Bonnie spotted movement behind one of the trees. She blurted a warning yell that roused the camp to action. The coffee spilled into the fire and hissed; the skillet with the eggs that Blanche had dropped clanged as it fell against a rock. There was a call from officers to "halt," and in a split-second, possemen stood in the open in a ring around the camp.

The call was answered by gunfire, and the Iowa officers quickly were introduced to the speed with which Clyde and

W. D. could get their Browning Automatic Rifles into action. Bonnie — and even Buck and Blanche — took up weapons.

The possemen were shooting, but the returning fire drove them back into the trees. I am sure that many of the rabbit-hunting farmers, who had come for a little excitement, already had had their fill of it.

Just as suddenly as the firing was taken up, the trapped fugitives made a dash for one of the cars. Clyde was at the wheel as the car started to make a run for it. But possemen, with a single target to worry about, were riddling it. A bullet caught Clyde in the arm, causing a jerk that sent the car barging into a stump, crumpling its left front wheel. Again, the wounded among the fugitives were told to "make a run for it," and, just as quickly, under covering fire from W. D.'s B.A.R., they made it to the sedan they'd stolen at Perry a short time before. But that car, too, was riddled. It was an easy target. The fugitives realized they could not get out with the car. Not a window glass remained. They piled out and scrambled for any cover they could find.

It was obvious now the fight was going to the possemen. Clyde, W. D., and Bonnie dashed toward a wooded area, distracting the posse. But the officers still were getting covering fire from Buck and even from Blanche, who were partially hidden by a stump. Blanche shrieked as Buck took the first of the bullets he would stop in the seconds that followed. Blanche handed him another clip of bullets, but they could not stop the hot fire of the possemen closing the ring on them. Two more slugs found Buck Barrow's back, and finally he slumped down, unable to fire any more. Blanche was hysterical, yelling "Don't die, Daddy! Don't die!"

The other phase of the bloody war that July morning in Iowa was the near hand-to-hand combat between W. D., Clyde, and Bonnie and the possemen blocking their path out. Deputy Sheriff Rags Riley of Polk County tried to rush them as they paused to catch their breath and help the faltering Bonnie through the woods. Clyde — his left sleeve a crimson ribbon and his arm useless — took aim and fired at Riley. The deputy dropped, with a wound in his forehead that stunned the farmers and caused them to hesitate just long enough to miss their opportunity. But — in one of those surprising things that sometimes happens in gunfights — Riley was barely wounded. He slapped his hand on his forehead, and brought back a bloodstain. But he emptied his weapon at the fleeing prey until all three were lost from his view.

Now, as Blanche was pleading, cursing, and moaning in fear that her man was dying, the posse closed in on them. Buck slumped as a fourth and fifth bullet drilled into his back. Blanche yelled "Don't shoot him any more. You've killed him already. Don't die, Daddy!" In a defiant gesture, she raised her weapon to fire, but it was half-hearted. A shot struck the weapon and it was blown from her hand.

In a split second, a physician from Des Moines — Dr. H. W. Keller, on National Guard duty — made a daring rush at the pair. He held the muzzle of his rifle on Buck Barrow's chest and kicked the pistol from the pale hand that held it. Other possemen restrained Blanche, who struggled like a caged tiger to be near Buck.

Blanche still was wearing her dark sunglasses, protection to her eyes. In her riding boots and corded riding pants, her red hair tousled from a night of sleeping out, and having been interrupted in her preparation of breakfast, she was a pathetic figure in her moment of arrest. Buck, she was sure, was dying.

The officers had captured only two of the Barrow Gang — certainly the mildest of the gang. The other three were still eluding the posse, despite the certainty of every officer that they had no way out. In fairness to the lawmen, their numbers were not nearly so large when the makeup of the posse is considered. A number were farmers who were as much hindrance as help. And there was also the ever-present danger of firing on one another that made caution necessary. And caution at a time like this invariably proves very costly.

Word spread quickly in Dexfield Park and the towns and cities around Iowa. We received word in Dallas while Clyde, Bonnie, and W. D. were still no doubt trapped within the twenty-acre park enclosure.

I heard later from Bonnie's family the stories she told them about how all those manhunters came so close to ending the Barrow Gang crime spree for once and all.

Clyde took advantage of the activity surrounding the capture of Buck and Blanche to run over a bridge to a house through the woods in hopes of finding an escape car. W. D., his eyes blinded by blood from a head wound, clung to Bonnie, helping her as he could through the biting briars and thorny brush to a hiding place at the river. They waited for Clyde to return, worrying that he might not be able to return at all. And they surely felt naked without weapons that were discarded when their ammunition ran out.

They could hear firing in the distance. They were certain now that Clyde had met more of the posse. But after some moments, as planes now began to circle overhead, they heard a hissing signal. At first, believing this was a ruse by officers to find them, W. D. and Bonnie chose not to respond. Then Clyde emerged, crawling toward them through the brush and grass, now embracing Bonnie softly, and cringing from the pain of his own arm that was wounded and useless.

Clyde had found a car but also had found possemen waiting at the bridge — or precisely, where the bridge had been. The officers had wrecked the bridge so it could not be crossed by a car. There was only one way out now — they had to swim the river.

Officers had more opportunities to stop them at the river as each of the three made their way alone, leaving pinkish bloodstains on the water. But the bullets merely whizzed close by them, except for one that grazed Bonnie and sent her under the surface for a time. Since Clyde was disabled, it was W. D. who finally rescued the faltering Bonnie and dragged her to the opposite side of the river and into a heavy growth of shrubbery that hid their movements.

Clyde left W. D. and Bonnie behind while he made his way through a cornfield tall with summer's growth of light green stalks in rows and onto a clearing on the other side, where three men were listening to the gunfire that had been echoing beyond the river. They found themselves transfixed with the sight of Clyde Barrow holding a pistol on them. They had no way of knowing that the weapon probably would not have fired so soon after it had been submerged in the crossing of the river.

The three men, farmer Valley Fellers, his son Marvel, and their neighbor Walter Spillers, heard the desperate Clyde panting and demanding a car, quick.

Fellers did not argue the point. He indicated the Plymouth sedan in the yard. Clyde whistled for W. D. to come ahead with Bonnie. The youngest member of the gang emerged from the cornfield, cradling Bonnie in his arms. Clyde ordered the farmers to help put her in the car. Fellers helped with the movement but blurted, "The girl is dead."

In a moment, the car was headed out of the farmyard onto a little-used road. The sheriff's office was notified as fast as Fellers could sprint to the road and yell to a passing posseman. A general alarm was telephoned to neighboring towns and cities. Hardly had the telephoning begun than a report came from Dale, a town fourteen miles to the northwest of Dexter, that someone had seen the fleeing Barrow car speeding through.

But by the time authorities reached Dale, word was telephoned back to Dexter that the fugitives now had passed Panola, eight miles beyond Dale. Airplanes were sent up. The word was spread. But the trail now was getting colder. Somewhere they had taken a turn off the main road. And perhaps they never reached the main road at all. Reports have a way of growing when times are tense, and fiction and fact are acted upon with equal intensity.

Country lanes around Panola were scoured after one report. And at Polk City, twenty miles out of Des Moines, George Allbright was robbed at gunpoint — with that gun that now might have been ready to fire. The bandits took Allbright's Chevrolet and dropped off the Plymouth that turned out to be the one taken from Valley Fellers at the farm a short time before.

That was something to go on. Five posses were dispatched from Des Moines to make a barn-by-barn search in case the fugitives had taken refuge in that vicinity after they had changed cars at Polk City. Officers reasoned that Clyde would need treatment for his shattered arm, which had appeared useless and painful when he brandished the weapon. The girl, too, might by dying. Radio broadcasts emphasized that the Barrow Gang was probably searching for a doctor.

An insurance man named Hugo Saggau at Dennison, ninety miles northwest of Dexter, reported that a young man walked into his place of business and asked where he could find a doctor. And a druggist in the same Iowa town said a "highly nervous" man bought a hypodermic needle in his store and rushed out.

The reports offered hope for a time. Certainly they created excitement. But nothing came from any of the searches, though some were major operations. The Chief of Iowa State Agents, Park A. Findley, personally cruised over a wide area of the state — and many counted some two hundred cars taking to the highways and roads just waiting for his plane to signal with a tipped wing that the Barrows had been spotted. U.S. Marshal Fred Hird, FBI Agent O. C. Dewey, and Adjutant General Charles Grahl of the Iowa National Guard all appeared within minutes after a report had placed the fugitives in a ravine near Sutherland, northwest of Dexter and about fifty miles from the Minnesota state line.

Clyde — despite his shattered left arm — apparently was still master of the three things he knew best: he could drive like the wind, tirelessly, without sleep and without relying on the main roads to get him where he wanted to go, and he could turn back and throw a searching party off its course. He found ways to forage, from little farm gardens if it came to that, for food. And he could stage small holdups for the minor amount of cash and supplies he needed, knowing that not more than half of his escapades would be reported, because his victims would be fearful he might return. Add to that the willingness of the three, Clyde, W. D., and Bonnie, to forego whiskey that could make them slow to react in tight situations.

Any country lane led to a creek that offered a chance to wash themselves and a remote area where their car could be hidden from view while they snatched a few hours sleep in a ravine or a lonely wood. And when they required news about where the official pursuit of the Barrows was going, they could snatch a newspaper from a rural mailbox and generally find a story about themselves.

While the major searching efforts were proceeding in Iowa, the three were apparently near Colorado City en route to

Denver; and they might have proceeded to Denver except for a newspaper account that reported falsely that "a woman believed to be Bonnie Parker checked into a Denver hospital with serious wounds."

It was also apparently from newspaper accounts that Clyde and Bonnie learned that Buck, as expected, had died of his gunshot wounds and that Blanche — now described in the newspapers as "a Barrow Gang gun-moll" — was imprisoned.

It was during this period, after Clyde's wounds had healed so that he could drive without severe pain, that W. D. Jones parted company with the older companions who had been his idols when he joined them in December of 1932, eight eventful months before. Through much of his time with Clyde and Bonnie, his identity continued to baffle almost every police department and all lawmen outside of Dallas. But he would turn up again later. He had, in fact, been a valuable young apprentice. But now he had had enough of sleeping fitfully in ravines, listening uneasily for any breaking twig that might signal another gunfight at a second's notice. He may have gained the wisdom to know that Clyde and Bonnie were only going to get themselves killed one day, and, quite surely, himself with them if he continued. His picture never was flashed across the pages of newspapers in the fashion of the famous Clyde and Bonnie. Perhaps he could go it alone, now that he had learned the outlaw game. One morning he was gone.

To pick up on our story at the time when officers surrounded Buck and were restraining the sobbing and hysterical Blanche, word of the capture flashed around the world. Buck was removed to King's Daughters Hospital in Perry, Iowa, and kept under tightest guard. Security was as complete as it could be made there — for the rumor was out that Clyde and W. D. and Bonnie would burst in with guns blazing and spring Buck from his deathbed, right from under the noses of the armed guards. Bars went up over the hospital doors; Buck's room was locked securely. Officers stood guard in the room and outside it and in the halls and on the porches.

Blanche was removed from the Dallas (Iowa) County Jail at Adel, which lacked quarters for women prisoners, to a lockup in Des Moines. True to her husband and her companions in a criminal role that she had unwillingly adopted, Blanche stubbornly denied everything. The information she gave at the outset was designed only to confuse and mislead her interrogators.

She spoke of a companion in crime named "Blythe" — and made her fictional character so realistic that a man by that name was picked up by officers at a tiny oil town in Oklahoma called Snomac. That Blythe convinced officers he had no part in the Barrow crime spree — though he admitted having had some brushes with the law in Oklahoma. Blanche thought it was a delightful joke that she could cause such furor just by dropping a made-up name.

Officers took the better part of Buck's clearer periods to learn from him what they could of crimes in various states. Bob Alcorn and I went up from Dallas to assist and to learn what we could. Peace officers came in from Missouri and Arkansas to clear some of their cases.

He was quick to take blame for the shooting of Marshal Humphrey at Alma, Arkansas, and even appeared to recognize Deputy Salyers, who traded shots with two gunmen after Humphrey fell dead in the shootout.

"Remember me, Buck?" Salyers asked the dying man.

"Sure do. I was about to blow you off when you ran for that barn. That was the smartest thing you ever did," Buck said softly. Salyers was convinced from that time that it was Buck, not Clyde, who killed Marshal Humphrey. But remember, Buck was beyond further punishment. In a few days, at most, he would be dead and he knew it. To get some of the murders charged to him might be the only thing left that he could do for his brother, Clyde.

Detective DeGraff wanted more details about the Joplin affair; Sheriff Tom Bash of Jackson County, Missouri, hoped Buck would shed light on the shooting of his men at Platte City. Sheriff Coffey, completely recovered, also came up from Platte City, and so did Prosecutor Clevenger.

At first, Clevenger got no cooperation at all from Blanche. Later, after cooling for a time in jail, and perhaps embittered that Clyde and Bonnie had left Buck to his fate along with her, Blanche cleared up some minor points:

Yes, she said, the gang had been living on the few dollars taken in a great many robberies of small stores and filling stations, many of which apparently weren't even reported to authorities. And, certainly yes, both Clyde and Bonnie knew they were going to be shot and killed one day — but they knew they would be electrocuted if they gave themselves up. They intended to stick together and face death together when it came. And, yes, except in the past few weeks, they had practiced their shooting every two days in remote areas.

Among the crowds of people who flocked into Perry, Iowa, were the mothers of Clyde and Bonnie, Clyde's sister, Billie, and his younger brother, L. C. They had set out driving at 1 A. M. Tuesday from West Dallas; they had driven all through Tuesday and arrived at noon on Wednesday when they were admitted to Buck's bedside. In their opinion, Buck appeared clear headed enough on Wednesday but became foggy as his condition noticeably worsened Thursday.

I learned from members of the family that Buck's mind became confused. He seemed to believe that L. C. actually was Clyde and Billie was Blanche. He raved and begged Clyde to "run and take Blanche . . . don't leave her . . . she's hungry . . ."

The mothers at their time of distress had each other. They waited in their rooms in a hotel across the street or on the porch of the hospital, where they begged officers for any information they might have on the health of Bonnie and Clyde when they were last reported seen.

Anything they might have learned about Bonnie's health would have been disappointing at that time. The last reliable report came from the farmers who had helped W. D. load her into the car that Clyde was stealing at gunpoint after the episode in Dexfield Park. The farmer was certain at that time she was either dead or about to die.

After a pitiful day and night of calling for Clyde and his wife, Blanche, Buck Barrow was pronounced dead at 2 P. M. on Saturday, July 29, 1933.

Blanche remained all the while in jail at Des Moines. Buck's body would be returned to West Dallas for the funeral, and Blanche would miss it.

Now, instead of expecting Clyde and Bonnie to crash in with guns blazing to steal Buck away from the hospital, the rumors had it that Clyde planned to attend the funeral in disguise. So strong was the rumor that even though he positively did not attend, and would hardly have been in a condition to attend, some accounts persist to this day that Clyde was at the funeral in the disguise of an old woman.

The fact is, every person at the funeral was identified or recognized. Not more than fifty people gathered at the Sparkman-Holtz-Brand Chapel for brief services in Dallas on July 31, 1933. Most of these were family, relatives, neighbors, peace officers, and newspapermen. The Rev. Frank P. Dailey of Cedar Valley Baptist Church read some scripture and a prayer, and then the ceremony moved in a small procession to the West Dallas Cemetery for the burial. You may see the myth printed again that Clyde was among those in attendance. He was not. I would have known him, despite a beard, despite a bonnet he might have worn, or under any other disguise. We were, believe it or not, on the lookout for just such a stunt.

But I did not feel at all well that circumstances had turned out this way for Buck, to be buried without having Blanche among the few people who mourned his passing. I felt a deep pain for the parents, Henry and Cumie Barrow, and Buck's sisters and young L. C. The dirt was piled on Buck's grave and it was over just like that. He was thirty.

Blanche had been so right. If she allowed Buck to go to Clyde, just for a visit, Clyde would be no good for him. He would slip right into his old ways and there would be trouble and there wouldn't be anything he could do about it. Buck had said he "knew better than to get tied in with Clyde."

But now, many miles from where the hollow goodbyes were being said, Blanche was in jail. She would soon go before a judge and plead guilty to charges brought against her for the Missouri escapes, and she would be sentenced to ten years in prison.

Even so, and without defending her, the worst crime committed by that farm girl with the red hair, who was not bad looking at all, was that she loved Buck Barrow.

IX

A Mystery Solved

AFTER BUCK was buried, we waited for weeks before turning up more workable clues. During this period I was put on another case that was causing quite a stir.

Sometime before I'd joined Smoot as a deputy, a young man named Abe Schreiber, the son of a well-to-do Galveston businessman, and his fiancée Pauline Corman were found shot to death. It was a grisly case. Their bodies were left in underbrush alongside Overton Road outside Dallas; the young man's body was draped over a fence, as though he had struggled as he was dying. Their jewelry and other possessions had been stripped from them. My records show that this had happened on June 27, 1931. The story had been in all the papers, but apparently the case had gone unsolved. I doubt that even the families of the young victims believed they would ever be cleared; they would go through their lives without knowing what had happened to Abe and Pauline.

On a Wednesday evening, more than two years later — actually August 30, 1933 — another beautiful young girl and her young boyfriend were killed in much the same fashion. Kathryne Prince had been out with Mace Carver the night before, and she had failed to return home. The Carver boy had been found near death by a farmer between Dallas and the

Mesquite community which lay just to the East. At Parkland Hospital, in a state of delirious semiconsciousness, he managed to get his story out in short bits between painful pauses. To the doctor's suggestion that he needed to save his strength, the boy said it was important to him that he tell officers what had happened; he was concerned for Kathryne Prince, the girl he intended soon to marry, and he wanted us to bring her to him to let him see for himself she was all right.

She was not all right. At this moment a search was on for her around the Pleasant Mound farming neighborhood between Mesquite and Dallas. It wasn't like her to remain out late; and she always came home, her parents insisted.

Carver told of going with her Wednesday evening to visit her girl friend in Oak Cliff and, finding her friend not at home, going to a church service together instead. After that they drove around, stopping by the place he worked at Crystal Ice Company on Second Avenue in South Dallas. He told his employers he would be at work at midnight as usual, that he was taking Kathryne home. He did not make it.

"We had stopped on Ash Lane and two Negroes appeared at the car, holding a gun on us. They didn't say anything, but one opened my door and the other opened the door on Kathryne's side. And we were crowded in together in the front seat; the one on the right was holding the gun on us. He ordered Kathryne to sit on my lap and the other young black man began driving, and they argued which road they should take. I suppose they drove for fifteen minutes, though it seemed longer, and I recognized the area as somewhere near Balch Springs, about two miles from where they first came upon us. Then they told us we'd have to get out of the car. At first I thought they wanted only our money. I told them I had a watch, a seventeen-jewel Elgin; I gave them that.

"But I was ordered to walk toward the woods, and I noticed that the other one was standing with Kathryne alongside the car. Then the one following me said, "Turn around." And when I did, he shot me. Then I think he must have shot me again. They were very black. They did not have coats, but the one with pistol wore a hat and suspenders — he must have been six feet tall."

By the time the boy had told his story, he was too weak to sign the statement. Dr. J. H. Stephenson, who was superintendent of the hospital at the time, asked him if he could muster his strength to make an ''x.'' He did that and lapsed into unconsciousness. He died soon afterwards.

The morning dawned hot on Thursday. I told Smoot I would like to make my own investigation; several other deputies and police of Dallas and Mesquite had joined in the search for the missing girl. I headed out alone in my Model A roadster to the spot where the young man Mace Carver had been found dying, some distance away from the school where the 1930 Chevy he had driven now was parked, just off Mesquite Highway.

In those days, this was all cotton country, and this was cotton picking time on that blackland that is about the most fertile soil in Texas. I headed out alone, to see if I could get some ideas together and figure this one out. Two assailants had caught two lovers parked in a car — a common enough occurrence. It had to be somebody who lived close around; that was my idea. I kept on driving, past fields of cotton where everybody in the fields dressed monotonously the same, the men in blue denim overalls and cheap and faded blue shirts, and there were black women who wore red bandanas on their heads. If you've seen one cotton field in picking time in Texas you've seen them all.

''Wait just a damned minute,'' I said to myself, and backed the car for a better look at something that I'd only half noticed. Something didn't look just right. Two men in one field were wearing white shirts; one had suspenders and a hat, like the clothes Carver had said his assailant wore — and you don't see town clothes like that in a cotton patch.

I stopped the car and walked straight to them. They pulled no cotton sack behind them. ''Boys, I'm looking for a missing girl — and I'm going to have to talk to you awhile. Mind if you come with me to the car?'' I asked them.

The young men were nervous, but I couldn't interpret anything from that. Naturally, when I told them I was a sheriff's deputy, they would express some normal surprise at ''the Law'' talking to them. I couldn't let them go without taking them for interrogation; the clothes fit the only description we had. I put the cuffs on them and set out to look for some help. "Let's drive," I told them.

I rolled up to where the city detectives Will Fritz and J. T. Luther were standing and told them what I'd found. "This is Bluitt and Thurman Burkley. They're dressed awful well to be out picking cotton, and they forgot their cotton sack. Would you like to talk to one of 'em?"

Bluitt, the older of the two, stayed with Fritz. I put Thurman back in the car and we started to drive.

"Tell me what you've been doing, Thurman," I said.

"Did you find the girl yet?" he wanted to know.

"Do you know where she is?"

He looked puzzled, unsure of how much we knew.

"Your brother's going to tell if you don't," I tried.

He thought that over. Then he pointed, "It's over thisa-way."

Then he started spilling out his story, how he had left the City Market on Pearl Street about 9:30 Wednesday night after picking up a couple of watermelons in his brother Jarvis's car, and he and Bluitt drove Jarvis on to his house, and Jarvis let them take the car when he got out.

He described how he and his brother drove to a little side road and ran up on a car driving slowly, and he noticed a boy and a girl in the car. He said Bluitt passed the car, and then the car behind stopped and cut its lights, so Bluitt stopped and they both walked back to the car with the gun to see if they could get a little excitement.

His account from that point was very much like the statement Mace Carver had struggled to give at Parkland Hospital.

"We got out and walked back to where they were, got into their car, and made the girl sit on the man's lap, and we drove around for twenty minutes or so and stopped. I made the man walk out into the timber a little piece from the road . . . and I shot him twice with the pistol I got from Jarvis. I left the man out there where I'd shot him and drove out to that field right about there, and . . ."

"You raped her, you both raped her, and you shot her" I finished.

"Nossir," the boy said. "Bluitt shot her. I shot the man, but Bluitt shot the girl."

He led me to Kathryne Prince's body, in a large field of tall Johnson grass. She had been badly abused and beaten before she was shot. The searching parties had been this way before, and now a crowd of farmers and searchers was not more than a few hundred yards away, walking briskly toward us.

"Now, Thurman, I'm going to have to keep those farmers from killing you. They've got guns and they've got pitchforks. Head straight for the car and we're going to take off."

The few dozen farmers already had assembled in the area. I saw Will Fritz with Bluitt Burkley heading for a nearby house, so I took Thurman there. And after both boys had agreed they would stick to the stories they had told us separately, we did the cautious thing and took the brothers quickly away to the city jail.

The farmers were white and hard-working types whose worst fears about their Negro neighbors now had been realized. Brought up in the country, a long way from the certainty that law would finally prevail, they had a strong impulse, as they talked things over among themselves, to take the law into their own hands. And the more they talked, the braver they got, and you just can't allow such a thing. I certainly wasn't intending to let them take my prisoner, and the sooner I had that boy in jail downtown the sooner I'd feel comfortable about it. Even the girl's father, I think, had a shotgun. And he was a better man than that, but you have to consider the agony the man was going through, too.

The brothers were placed in the city jail, and then, for a short time, I learned what it is like to be an Instant Hero.

I never cared for playing the publicity game, and Will Fritz, one of the best lawmen I've ever known, didn't either. He gave a story to the papers that related the facts as they had happened.

City officials and the city police department had been catching a great deal of flak in the newspapers the week before, when some Dallas officers barged into a house, the wrong house, it turned out, without a warrant. Now they had a lawsuit on their hands. So, I suppose, they were under a lot of pressure to take credit for the Burkley brothers' arrest. The city manager was quick to find someone from the press to point out what a tremendous job the city police had done. I knew he was getting all the mileage he could out of the arrest coming a day after the crime had been committed.

I knew, too, that Smoot would want the prisoners removed to the county jail; he probably needed some credit for the sheriff's department, too.

Considering how much the city fellows wanted to keep the Burkleys, it wasn't surprising to me that when I dropped by city hall to see if the farmers from Pleasant Mound were causing any ruckus, I wasn't permitted inside. And there was another reason: the mob there might get dangerous.

There's no tougher job for lawmen than standing off a group of hotheads. It had become fairly clear to everyone that Mace Carver would die; it was only a matter of time. In his condition, with spinal cord severed and a terrible head wound, too, death probably would be welcomed. The farmers in the Pleasant Mound neighborhood had tremendous respect for the parents of both Kathryne and Mace. I can't imagine what thoughts would go through my own mind if I were in the place of the parents.

We succeeded in getting the prisoners transferred to the county jail without incident. But the farmers descended on us there. Smoot had several of us mill around with them, engage them in conversation, and keep them from having the same idea all at once to storm the jail and get the Burkley boys.

One thing played into our hands: the evidence was airtight in this case; even their brother, Jarvis, confirmed the first part of their story, about Bluitt and Thurman dropping him at the house and taking the car, with the gun, on a joy ride in search of excitement. The parents didn't make an effort to alibi for the boys either. They were distressed that two of their sons had come to this, and that didn't make their sadness lighter. But the fact that the grand jury was in session and was prepared to return murder indictments against the brothers by 9:00 that evening — less than twenty-four hours after the deed — diffused the bitterness of the mob. But I still wouldn't relish facing something like that again.

I'd been lucky.

And the luck held out again. A few evenings later, the pangs of conscience were stirred in the brothers by a visit from the family's minister. He came out of their cell with a request that they'd like to make another statement, confessing to the unsolved slaying two years earlier of Abe Schreiber and his young girl friend, Pauline Corman.

Instead, we waited until midnight and took them under heavy guard to the general area where that double murder had occurred. The brothers took it from there; they told the story without missing a single detail — and invited us to take them to their house where they could find some articles of clothing and jewelry they'd taken from the victims.

But try as they did to dig up a gold watch that the father of Abe Schreiber had told me he'd like to recover for special sentimental reasons, the boys could do no more than give us the place where they'd buried it.

Some time later, I understand, one of the city officers went out and found it and returned the heirloom to its rightful owner.

In due course, a trial found the brothers guilty of two counts of murder each. They were sentenced to die in the electric chair. And it fell on me to stand with them as they approached the chair.

I have often wondered how such a case might have been handled today, if I had been forced by the Supreme Court to read them their rights, to get them a lawyer who would advise them to keep their murders quiet, and to make the state prove that they murdered when they had, in fact, ruthlessly murdered both witnesses in each case by a barbaric act committed in the dark. I know the answer to that: there'd have been no earthly way we could have obtained a conviction. They could have gone out on that road again, and again, and there would have been no witnesses, again.

The trial would come several months later. In the meantime, other cases still weren't solved, and there wasn't much time to rest on our small achievement. We arrested the brothers on a Thursday, and it was business as usual again on Friday morning.

In the late summer of 1933, W. D. Jones parted company with Clyde and Bonnie.

X

Machine Gun Kelly Was a Piker

BONNIE AND Clyde escaped from Dexfield Park in July of 1933 and didn't surface again until November. But in those summer and fall months while I was waiting for clues, I had no lack of other cases to work on.

The early 1930s, particularly in the Southwest, were times filled with a bloody wave of crime that the tabloids and sensational "Police Story" magazines thrived on. In these months, besides the Burkley brothers, George "Machine Gun" Kelly and Harvey Bailey were among our headliners. They were small fry compared to Clyde and Bonnie, but they caused Sheriff Schmid plenty of trouble, and I was glad to help solve the case of Bailey's jailbreak.

Kelly and Bailey were kidnappers. I maintain even today that kidnapping not only is a cowardly crime but an ineffective way for a criminal to make money. Whether or not it is true that crime doesn't pay, kidnapping surely has been the least profitable of all crime.

"Machine Gun" Kelly and Harvey Bailey on June 17, 1933, had cut down four officers in the Kansas City Union Station massacre — all in an effort to prevent their friend Frank Nash from returning to prison. In the gunfire, Nash was killed along with the officers. This was a notable case of misguided friendship, but it showed something of the ruthlessness of Kelly and Bailey.

The same Kelly and Bailey a short time later, on July 22, 1933, caught Oklahoma City millionaire oilman Charles F. Urschel playing bridge on his porch with a friend named Jarrett. The kidnappers strong-armed them into a waiting car and drove — as Urschel later was to recall — about fifteen hours.

Jarrett was freed after only an hour, but as some old-timers may recall, the kidnappers originally demanded $250,000 for Urschel's safe return. The figure that was agreed upon after negotiation was $200,000, which was finally paid in Missouri.

To recap the story in a brief form, Urschel was freed, and the investigation to learn where he had been held and to catch the kidnappers occupied some of the Southwest's best lawmen as well as the FBI. Fingerprints in the FBI's old Southern Railway Building on Washington's Pennsylvania Avenue confirmed every lawman's initial hunch — that the kidnapping was the work of Kelly and Bailey. The problem now was to find them.

Urschel, though blindfolded during all of his travel to prevent his knowing where he had been held, was remarkable for things he remembered during his eight-day ordeal as a captive. He recalled the mineral taste of the water from a well at the northwest of the rude tenant farm shack where he was kept, the squeaky well rope as the water was drawn, the thunder and rain one day, and the smell that comes in the air in the country when rain breaks a dusty drouth. But more important was his recollection of the time an airplane regularly passed over the house at 9:45 each morning and about 5:45 each afternoon. That information dovetailed with some other facts turned up in the investigation; it proved to be the downfall of the kidnappers and more than a dozen people who befriended them.

Machine Gun Kelly's wife, Kathryn Thorne Kelly, was a daughter of a Mr. James Emory Brooks and Ora L. Brooks. But they had been divorced, and Mrs. Brooks was the present Mrs. Robert G. Shannon of Paradise, Texas, in southwestern Wise County, just to the northeast of Fort Worth. Kathryn herself had been married to a Lonnie Fry of Asher, Oklahoma, and after having a daughter, who was fourteen at the time of the kidnapping, had been married for a time also to one Charles Thorne of Coleman, Texas. Thorne had been found dead, under circumstances that were considered mysterious even as the coroner labeled the death a suicide because a note had been found that had Thorne's name under a message that said he "could not live with or without Kathryn."

With those marriages behind her, Kathryn married a former inmate of the New Mexico state prison named George Kelly Barnes who was, at least since the Kansas City Massacre, known as "Machine Gun Kelly."

Any case involving a prominent rich man develops hundreds of leads that have to be checked out laboriously in many areas. Meteorologists outlined areas within hundreds of miles of Oklahoma City that had received drenching rainfall on the day Urschel remembered rain.

Scheduled airline activity — in those days when very few schedules were flown — was checked. A flight from Fort Worth to Amarillo departed at 9:15 A. M. each day — but on one day it was routed off the direct line to skirt a storm. Lawmen boarded the plane to have a look at the countryside that would be directly below the plane at 9:45 A. M. and 5:45 P. M.

While the fact that the airline flew over the Shannon farm, where Kathryn Kelly's mother lived, at approximately those times would not prove anything by itself, investigators decided the farm was worth an on-the-ground look. On August 10, a lawman posing as a salesman visited the farm and decided the general layout fit Urschel's description. When water was drawn from a well, the well rope squeaked, and, also as Urschel remembered, the water had a mineral taste.

One mile and a half distant was the farm of Armon Shannon — old man Shannon's son. The younger Shannon admitted that he had seen both George and Kathryn Kelly on the day of the reported kidnapping, but, he said, they had only been visiting and had left. But two days later, after keeping watch on the place in hopes that Kelly would return, a raid was made quietly at the farmhouse by local, federal, and state officers. Harvey Bailey was asleep on a cot outside, near a getaway car that was pointed outward, and a machine gun and two pistols were nearby.

Bailey surrendered meekly without making a move toward any of his weapons. Urschel was brought in, and he confirmed that the rude farmhouse had been his prison. Along with Bailey, almost $1,200 in currency was seized — and about $800 of this bore the secret markings placed on the kidnap money before the payoff. The Shannons also were brought in — Mr. and Mrs. Robert G. Shannon and Armon Shannon — to be charged with harboring the fugitives.

They implicated the Kellys and also another notorious character of that day, Albert Bates. Bates was soon in the custody of Denver police; he had carried $660, and this too contained some of the ransom bills.

Bailey was brought to the Dallas County jail for safekeeping on contract with the federal government, which was a usual procedure.

To put the Machine Gun Kelly and Harvey Bailey story in the context of the time, the case in no way could keep other criminals off the front pages. All too much was happening. Bonnie and Clyde still were operating, and lesser lights such as Woodrow Underhill and Pretty Boy Floyd occasionally would make a splash. There was more than enough for all of the undermanned law enforcement agencies to work on.

As for the job I was hired to do — delivering subpoenas and keeping an eye on the record keeping of the office — that role was long gone. As long as so many crimes were being committed that needed investigating, that would be the role I would assume — and I suspect that Smoot had this figured out all along.

Then, on the morning of September 4, on Labor Day Weekend, Bailey made a break from his sixth-floor cell of the Dallas County Jail. The break was accomplished with suspicious ease. Jailer Tresp had found himself staring at the business end of a long-barrelled .44 Smith & Wesson, and he must have known that Bailey would not hesitate to use it. A good lawman, expecting to be killed under those circumstances anyway, would have tried to stop Bailey, and I wondered why Tresp did not stand his ground there in the jail. But he did as he was ordered; he walked out with Bailey and headed north out of Dallas with Bailey's gun trained on him.

Even with the communication we had in those days, officers at Ardmore, Oklahoma, were alerted in time to catch Bailey and to free Tresp unscathed. Bailey moaned and cursed, but again he surrendered without ever having fired his weapon.

Sheriff Schmid was in Chicago at the time. Those of us who were both his friends and deputies knew he would take heat from the newspapers and the public for the jailbreak. Obviously the weapon and some hacksaw blades found in Bailey's cell had been smuggled inside — and Bailey had not had more than eight or ten visitors during his confinement. I made the rounds of pawn shops and hardware stores, looking for the source of the ancient .44 and the hacksaw blades that would cut through the hardest steel. And again I was lucky.

The four indentations on the cap of one of the cartridges taken from the pistol showed that Bailey had tried four times to fire the weapon and had not succeeded. It was easy now to see the reason for his rage. But he would be no immediate help in our search for accomplices who tried to set him free.

Two of the cartridges were .44 caliber but were designed for firing in a Colt instead of a Smith & Wesson. The other two were actually .38 caliber, though there is a chance Bailey had no opportunity to inspect the cartridges carefully while in his jail cell. The slight variation in size of the bullets invited the weapon to jam — otherwise, I am certain, Jailer Tresp would have died and so would one or more of the arresting officers.

At a hardware store on Exposition Avenue near Fair Park, a clerk said he had, indeed, sold hacksaw blades and an old .44 caliber long-barrel Smith & Wesson recently — four days before the break, it was — to a man he thought he could identify — and he had seen the man before at the county jail.

His identification was precise, though it made me sick that it happened: he readily identified a picture of Chief Jailer Tom Manion and a friend of Tom's, a butcher named Grover Bevill. Both, of course, protested their innocence.

"Bailey couldn't pay me enough to make me take a chance on looking through bars the rest of my life," Manion told reporters who were allowed to come up and see him behind bars. The old jailer had been a bodyguard for a former Dallas Mayor, Waddy Tate, and a law enforcement man practically all his life. The man had five kids, which doesn't excuse him at all, but that may have been a point when he saw an opportunity to share some of the ill-gotten gains of the Urschel kidnapping.

"I'm too smart a man to send a friend who could be identified to buy guns and hacksaw blades at a place where he could be identified," Manion went on. "Besides, I'd be endangering the life of my fellow jailers."

But the fact is, as later testimony revealed positively, the old jailer had done all those things. Further, he and Bevill were identified from photographs as the men who were seen conducting conversation with a man who was identified as Machine Gun Kelly on a road outside Dallas, four days before the Labor Day weekend break.

The early capture of Bailey removed much of the heat that would have fallen on Smoot. No matter who was to blame within the jail, the public would blame Smoot. That was natural; that's the way it is for the man in the top job. So Smoot was grateful I had quickly found the source of the weapon and the blades and through a stroke of luck had piled up evidence enough to convict the two men who were responsible for Bailey's break.

After a time in jail, Bevill thought about what had suddenly happened to him for his folly and detailed the entire account to federal officials. What was even more ironic, Bailey held such bitter feelings about being given a weapon that would not fire that he confirmed the story, to further embarrass Manion, that Kelly had made the arrangements, which were to have consisted of ten thousand dollars in payments to Manion and Bevill for springing Bailey — though Kelly had made only a small down payment.

Manion drew a two-year sentence at Leavenworth and a ten-thousand-dollar fine; Bevill, for his cooperation with federal authorities, got off lighter with only fourteen months.

Machine Gun Kelly and his wife Kathryn later surrendered without a struggle — the way John Dillinger had surrendered so many times. In this, they were pikers, compared to Clyde and Bonnie.

In all sixteen people drew sentences for their part in the Urschel kidnapping or for harboring the criminals. Manion had stupidly contributed to the notion held by many of the public that law enforcement officers cannot be entirely trusted. He let the department down, and, especially, he let down his family, which by some strange logic he thought he would be helping for turning a mad-dog killer out onto the streets again. His crime hardly paid for his trouble. Apparently he received only $250 of his promised payment.

As for Sheriff Schmid, he showed his gratitude to me in a most peculiar way.

"Ted," he said, "this escape business is going to stop. We're going to deliver Manion and Bevill to trial, and if they're sentenced, you'll personally take the prisoners to Leavenworth. In the meantime, you'll watch them."

It was hardly the assignment I would have chosen. But I did it.

And, just as he promised, he ran me up to Leavenworth to deliver the prisoners after they were sentenced.

"When I get back," I told Schmid, "I'd like to go full time on Bonnie and Clyde if it's all right with you."

Schmid said he'd have to think about that.

I believe he already had thought about it — and faked me into asking for the job.

XI

The First Ambush

BONNIE AND Clyde reappeared in the oil fields east of Dallas in November, 1933.

Though the promised "recovery" of the sorry economic conditions was more wishful optimism of the politicians and Main Street than reality that autumn, there was money to be made in the East Texas oil fields. Since the colorful wildcatter E. M. "Dad" Joiner had made his discovery well on Daisy Bradfield's farm, a "boom town" fever had swept a band of counties east of Dallas. Geologists who had thought Joiner crazy now were admitting there might really be an "ocean of oil" under the cotton fields and scrub timberland around Henderson, Kilgore, and other communities. But oil production outran demand, and the price of a barrel of oil tumbled to a half-dollar or even less. Restrictions were imposed to cut production and bring prices up and curtail the shameful waste.

Even so, enterprising people like Jim McMurray could do well enough. McMurray set up a little refinery near the Overton community at a crossroads called Arp, not far from Kilgore, where the oil derricks already were placed so close to each other, a man could almost leap from one derrick floor to another across the town.

The first nip of fall chill had turned the leaves to a brilliant palette of color on the morning of November 8, 1933.

On that morning a Ford V-8 coupe with an Oklahoma license plate appeared at McMurray's refinery. But the arrival was hardly acknowledged by the handful of truck drivers working at a loading rack outside the plant office.

Bonnie Parker, unknown to any of the drivers except as a name in the newspapers or the detective magazines, was dressed neatly as she got out of the car, looked around as any curious visitor might, and returned to the car.

In a short time, she returned with two men.

The truck drivers stopped abruptly when Clyde Barrow's command rang out, "Get your hands up!" The husky fellows complied with the order of the man wearing dark glasses; they were herded inside the refinery office.

McMurray and his plant manager, Ray Hall, seeing the muzzles of the weapons, had no choice except to hold their hands up too.

Someone apparently had tipped the bandits to the whereabouts of the "safe" — an eight-inch pipe protruding upward from the concrete floor, a padlock securing a hinged lid on it.

"O.K.," Clyde ordered gruffly, "give me the key or open it up."

McMurray denied having a key. Barrow did not choose to argue the point at all. A pair of shots rang out. Sparks flew as the bullet struck the lock and ricocheted — and the torn padlock fell to the floor. McMurray and Hall and the drivers looked on, wide-eyed and scared. Clyde bent down, pulled out a wad of greenbacks from the pipe, and backed out of the refinery office. "Make a false move and you're all dead," he barked, and the two men retreated to the Ford coupe where Bonnie had the motor running.

As the car departed, one of the drivers took down the license number: Oklahoma, 485-370. The brazen daylight robbery was immediately reported; roads were blocked routinely. And, again, there was no sign at all of the bandits. That alone would have convinced me that this was the work of Clyde and Bonnie. But I have never learned who had taken W. D. Jones's place as Clyde's sidekick on this one.

The license plate had been issued to a Waurika, Oklahoma, man named Glenn Daniels. He said his car had been stolen earlier in the month from a street in Wichita Falls, Texas, where he had parked it.

McMurray was unaware of the bandits' identities. He wasted no time getting to his home in Dallas, and he notified Sheriff Schmid, who directed him to me. The refinery was far out in the state, more than a hundred miles from Dallas, and certainly outside our Dallas County jurisdiction. But McMurray invited me to his house.

I listened to his story, how the bandits came with guns, how they ordered him to hold up his hands, how they demanded the key to the lock, and how he bluffed and said he had no key. And how he was scared out of his wits when the shots rang out and the lock was blown. He had lost between two and three thousand dollars to the bandits.

I heard his descriptions of the two men and the tiny "good-looking" woman, and I showed him photographs. "That's the woman," he said, though he had no idea who she was.

"You'd be willing to prosecute — to go into court and swear she was one of them?" I asked. He assured me he would do his duty. Then I turned over the picture of Clyde.

"That's *him*! He's the one who did all the talking and shot the lock off."

I showed him the name on the back of the picture. Though he had, apparently, never seen a photograph of Clyde Barrow before, the name sent a chill through him.

"No, Mr. Hinton," he said, "If it's all the same to you — forget I said that. He'd just come back and kill me. No — I'll just take my lumps and go about my business."

The take at McMurray's refinery was one of Clyde's largest scores up to this time. I was learning something of Clyde's habits: he never seemed to get more money than the amount of his immediate need. I'm certain that made sense to him; the longer he was a fugitive, the more likely was the chance that the bigger-money outfits had taken precautions against him. And, as one of his relatives told me, he had very little opportunity to spend money anyway.

In my off-duty hours, I found time to keep an eye on all of his old haunts in West Dallas. There couldn't have been more than five hundred adult people living in all of the region known as the "Bog" at that time, and I probably could have recognized all of them and called them by name. I didn't have to wait long this time to determine how Clyde had spent a fair slice of his money. Though even my good sources in West Dallas now were beginning to hold back on me — for it seemed half the people out there were either related to Clyde and Bonnie or were old school friends sympathetic to their predicament, if not to their choice of careers — reports of their activities would reach me, but always after the fact.

One of the strangest of these reports, or it seemed so at the time, was that the Barrow and Parker families already had been to a funeral home and arranged for the burials of Clyde and Bonnie. The report was in the newspapers, which by now were using their names as if they already were convicted of all the crimes attributed to them. The rumor had some substance in this instance. I was reasonably certain, even without asking the funeral home proprietors to violate their confidential relationship with the families, that besides squaring up the bill for Buck's funeral, Clyde would see arranging his own as entirely proper. He and Bonnie had chosen never to turn themselves in. There was only one way they would be stopped. They would die together some day.

Bob Alcorn was taking me into his confidence more now, and I was sharing my tips and observations with him. We were getting a reputation for working together, and my work with the criminal side of the sheriff's office now was occupying almost all my time. Someone else took up the process serving for which I'd originally been hired. I had a tip that W. D. Jones no longer was with Clyde and Bonnie. In such a case, if we didn't run into him in Dallas, I could be reasonably certain he'd be at a certain address in Houston. Alcorn took Ed Caster down to Houston and picked up W. D., who actually expressed happiness that he'd been found.

W. D. still was only seventeen, even after all the escapades that he had joined in with Clyde and Bonnie in December of 1932, when he idolized the bandits and learned the outlaw trade with them. It had been less than a year by the calendar, and he had seen five men die from gun blasts.

When W. D. was brought back to Dallas and was shown the photographs of himself with Bonnie, whom he called "Sis," and with Clyde, whom he called "Bud," he began telling a tale that filled in many of the pieces of the Barrow Gang's movements.

On November 16, 1933, Alcorn and I found a most willing subject when we interrogated W. D. He wanted to assure us, he said, that he had been a kidnap victim all along. Clyde and Bonnie took him unwillingly out of West Dallas, and when he found on his first try at robbing a store that he "just couldn't do such a thing," Clyde had called him a yellow punk and told him to steal a car and drive back to Dallas alone.

And that, he said, was how he came to get into Doyle Johnson's car at Temple, Texas. But he was so nervous and scared that he couldn't find the ignition to start the car, so Clyde finally got into the car himself and fired on Johnson when the car owner discovered him.

Further, he said, he was an unwilling participant in all the gang's crimes; whenever he tried to leave them to their own devious lives, they would catch him and threaten him. And once, when he had tried to leave, they chained him to a motel bedpost.

I didn't believe a word of it, but I was just as certain that a jury would be convinced.

W. D. was helpful in other ways, though most of his statement, which filled twenty-eight pages of typewriting, only confirmed what Alcorn and I already knew. The clear fact was that most of the Barrow depredations and their killings — except for the single shooting of Malcolm Davis, the Fort Worth officer who was killed on the porch of Lillie McBride's house in West Dallas on January 6, 1933 — were done outside of Dallas. This was a point that made our job as deputies more difficult than it might have been. We were among the few people who could recognize Clyde and Bonnie, but our jurisdiction ended at the county line. Except for swift runs in and out of Dallas occasionally to visit Mrs. Parker and Mrs. Barrow, Clyde and Bonnie had not yet become subjects of any concerted drive to stop them.

Even with his claims that he was not a willing partner, Jones gave us more information than he thought he was giving. We knew precisely when he had joined the outlaws trail, shortly before Christmas in 1932; we knew he was with them in Temple, when Doyle Johnson discovered them stealing the new car he was presenting to his wife and tried to stop them; and we had learned from Missouri and Iowa officers all we needed to know of their escapades in Joplin and Dexter.

Jones did not mean to convey his feeling of accomplishment — but he could not hide his satisfaction at having left West Dallas as a kid who'd never owned a new pair of shoes and was living now as a well-dressed man of the world. He had learned to look, at age seventeen, not at all the wide-eyed boy who idolized Clyde Barrow.

"It's hell out there, Mr. Hinton, just hell. Never sleep in a bed, never eat a good meal, always running scared, never knowing when a bullet is going to catch you. God, I'm glad to be in this jail. Don't ever make me leave it while Clyde's alive."

Jones showed seven scars, some of them still unhealed, that he said were the result of bullet wounds. He said in his statement that he was "knocked out cold" just about every time any officer was killed, though "I heard Clyde say he'd done it."

His story notwithstanding, Jones had become a deadly shot with the arsenal of weapons carried by the Barrows. Officers in three states already had told us of the "unidentified young man" who fired weapons alongside Clyde, Bonnie, and the late Buck Barrow. W. D. told of many hours of practice firing they did in remote hideouts in Arkansas and Missouri and in East Texas. The only part of his story we couldn't buy was that he had been held against his will.

Even so, the fact that Texas law at that time made conviction of anyone under eighteen difficult unless he freely admitted the crime assured Jones he would get off with a light sentence if he had to serve any time at all. He seemed more worried we'd run him out of jail than that we'd get him convicted of anything serious. His statement that he wanted to be held in jail "for protection against the vengeful Clyde

Barrow'' would look very good for him when it hit the newspapers. But we intended to report nothing to the newspapers — a policy that Alcorn taught me. We succeeded in having him held for more than a week without a word leaking to the press. This, of course, would be impossible today; but Jones insisted he didn't mind — he'd rather Clyde and Bonnie would never find out where he was hiding.

What we had hoped to gain from the long hours of attention we had given to Jones was anything we could learn of friends who had given them shelter or of any place they frequented on their occasional trips into Dallas or nearby counties.

On these points, he was less definite. He confirmed that Clyde had spoken of ''running into Ted Hinton'' on two or three occasions when he had tried to visit relatives in Dallas; and he mentioned that Clyde and Bonnie had met their families ''up near Grapevine, over in Oak Cliff on a high hill, and in some out-of-the-way places in East Texas where Clyde had lived when he was a small boy.'' But that wasn't much help.

It was a few days more before a couple of newspaper reporters would begin to ask questions of Sheriff Schmid about ''the rumor that you're holding one of the Barrow Gang incognito in your jail.'' Schmid denied it — and for a good reason.

I had a hunch of my own that Clyde and Bonnie ''just might'' be intending to pay a visit to their families. No one told me, though that is what everyone later presumed. I simply learned to detect actions of Mrs. Cumie Barrow. When I last saw her, she seemed to be more poker-faced and evasive than usual; that seemed to tell me she'd received some good news — and the only good news she would recognize was that she might see her Clyde very soon. But I had no way of knowing just where that would be.

A respected citizen named Charley Stovall ran a dairy farm operation near Sowers, northwest of Dallas. Charley had told me he was certain the Barrows on one or two occasions during the past months had visited on the seldom-used two-hundred-foot-wide right-of-way of a State Highway 15 that still was unpaved adjacent to his farm.

Stovall pointed out a spot where Clyde would park his car, blink his lights on and off, and a car bearing members of the Barrow and Parker families would soon draw up alongside. At least once, the farmer had seen them together there. He had been close enough to recognize them from photographs I had shown him and wise enough not to betray that he recognized them.

It would be completely accurate to say that Sheriff Schmid wanted nothing so much in the world as to capture Clyde Barrow and Bonnie Parker and to walk them down Main Street of Dallas to show the world what he'd done. If he could do that — which Alcorn and I repeatedly assured him he could not — Smoot felt his reelection would be assured. Hell, he might have become Governor if he could have made it happen that way, but the man was pipe dreaming. He refused to believe us when we assured him that Clyde would not give up, no matter how many men surrounded him. Too recently, I had seen what he'd done to the officers who had him surrounded and dead to rights in the trap at Joplin, Missouri, and in the park in Dexter, Iowa. Alcorn and I felt that he had already killed enough people; Alcorn failed to convince Smoot that he couldn't say merely, "Stop, in the name of the law," and slip handcuffs on Clyde Barrow.

Smoot said he was grateful for the tip, but he'd do it his way, and would we show him to the dairy farm up near Sowers? He said we'd park about a half-mile away, so as not to give away our position, and take our place just inside a fence alongside State Highway 15, where we would conceal ourselves until one of us recognized Clyde Barrow driving up. At that time, Smoot said, he would rise up, yell "Halt!" and we would just see Clyde recognize that he was outgunned and surrender.

Alcorn carried a Browning Automatic Rifle; Smoot and I had those tinny Thompson submachine guns, and Ed Caster carried a .351 repeating rifle.

We waited there crouched in the weeds for nearly an hour before the car approached. It was easy to recognize Bonnie at the wheel of the sedan, even in the dim light of dusk, because a car approaching from behind had their car bathed in light. I noticed Clyde at her side in the front seat. Some reports I have seen in later years have placed a second man in the back seat, but, as I recall clearly, only Bonnie and Clyde were in the car.

The approaching car was about seventy-five feet away when Smoot rose to his feet, and we all stood up quickly. Smoot yelled, "Halt!" which must have been the most futile gesture of the week. Bullets began to whizz at our feet and around us, coming from Clyde's side of the car. In a split second, the countryside must have shaken with the rattle of gunfire. If the car slowed, it was only the impact of our bullets answering the shots coming from the car as it passed us and moved on. In a desperate few seconds, we had shot out the windshield of the car, and we heard the crash of glass, as the car passed us; Bonnie was shooting, too, from the rear window, and Clyde had leaned over to steer the car away.

In the heat of the fire fight, I felt a bullet graze my arm, and then another. Both bullets passed through my coat without hurting me. We had managed to load the car full of holes, to knock out its windows and flatten a tire, but it only zigzagged crazily and disappeared. There could be no frustration quite like it.

"It was my fault, boys," Smoot said, dejectedly. "I should have listened to you fellows. And besides my bad judgment, my gun jammed. I didn't get a shot off."

All of us cursed our rotten luck. We knew we had poured a lot of lead into that car, though we weren't to know precisely how many shots had struck Clyde and Bonnie. We were certain that no one in the car could have avoided being hit somewhere. But our decision to park our car so far from where we now found ourselves, and the lack of any radio equipment, cost us valuable time in notifying anyone else of our failure. We walked as hurriedly as we could to the car to take up the chase, and learned — sadly — that Mrs. Charley Stovall, wife of the dairyman who lived a half-mile away from our ambush site, had been hit in the neck by one of the bullets. Luckily, the neck wound wasn't at all serious. But this incident taught us something: the weapons in use have a long range, and innocent people can die any time a gun battle erupts. I know this made an impression on me — an impression that made me cautious in choosing the time and place for any future gun battles.

By the time we reached a telephone to inform the office of our failure, we had reports that the car had been sighted. And a little later the pieces began to fit concerning their destination after the fugitives drove away with their rear tire flat.

Shortly after 7 P.M. that same evening, Clyde and Bonnie drove southward to the Fort Worth Pike west of Dallas and proceeded on to Jefferson Avenue, near the present site of Hensley Field and the Dallas Naval Air Station. They steered their car into the path of an oncoming Ford coupe occupied by Thomas R. James, a Forth Worth lawyer, and Paul Reich, also of Fort Worth. The two men were returning home after attending a Scottish Rite Reunion in Dallas.

Now they were forced to stop, and Clyde emerged from the bullet-riddled car, commanding James and Reich to ''get out of there!'' When James said, ''What is this anyway?'' Clyde emphasized his demand by firing a shotgun blast that tore a hole above the door, shattered both the side windows and windshield, and left both of his victims bleeding from cuts from the flying glass. James and Reich said later they were ''too frightened to feel anything.'' They heard Clyde tell Bonnie, ''Honey, get out and hold this gun on them,'' which left their assailant free to transfer some guns and other gear into the James car.

James and Reich were left standing on the highway, their heads bleeding. And alongside them was the car we had riddled.

As Clyde and Bonnie sped away in James's car, one man who had witnessed the entire episode approached in a car behind; Wade Collier had attended the same Scottish Rite Reunion and, like James and Reich, was returning home to Fort Worth. He took the two men to a doctor's office in Grand Prairie to have their wounds treated, and we sent a wrecker to tow the abandoned car with the bullet holes into Grand Prairie, which is about twelve miles west of Dallas.

Our examination of the car confirmed what we had suspected: we had hit one of them, or probably both of them. The front seat and the floor bore large blood smears, though we couldn't know at the time that both had been hit in the legs and knees, apparently without seriously hurting them. We found bed covers, pillows, medicines, lipstick, rouge, mirror, safety razor, knives and forks, a quantity of canned food, a sackful of pennies, and eleven different license plates, which could have helped them evade detection by officers who had only the reported license number for identification. And, as we learned to expect, they had the newest detective magazines, still recounting their exploits and escapes in Missouri and Iowa.

Closer examination told us more: they had fired at least ten shots at us, and apparently two .45s were used. We found ten shell casings in the car, five apiece fired from two different weapons.

Alcorn, Caster, and I had fired thirty rounds from a range of about seventy-five feet and closer, and the marks of at least seventeen were visible on the car, though the Ford V-8 body turned most of the fire from the Thompson submachine gun I had used, except, of course, those I had fired through the windows and at the tire. Definitely, I would not go hunting Clyde and Bonnie with a tommygun again. The B.A.R. that Alcorn carried was the only weapon that had any telling effect — and these bullets would go through the car and pass out on the opposite side.

This episode taught us why Clyde had a preference for Ford V-8s, though the car he swapped it for on Jefferson Avenue was a lesser machine, a 1931 four-cylinder coupe. At the time James and Reich had approached, Clyde was surely aware he would be spotted on the main road with a car so bullet riddled and running on a flat.

James recounted the story and said he was thankful to be alive. When Clyde failed to recognize where the ignition in his car could be located, he had asked, "All right . . . tell me how this works," and, James said, he replied, "Find it yourself."

In the cool of hindsight, and now aware that he had been facing the notorious Clyde Barrow, James considered himself lucky that Barrow didn't become impatient and shoot him.

"I'm lucky he found the ignition switch just when he did," James told me.

The 1931 four-cylinder coupe bearing Clyde and Bonnie was spotted in Corsicana shortly before daylight by a city police office there. The officer admitted that he started to take up the chase but then decided two things would happen to him, and neither prospect appeared good: either he would be outrun by Clyde and Bonnie, or he would catch them and have to draw his gun on them.

"I stopped and got a cup of coffee at an all night restaurant, and put in a call to Dallas that I saw Clyde Barrow in Corsicana," the officer told a local newspaperman.

The report was received in our office with understanding. But Alcorn and I knew that Clyde would not long be satisfied with that four-cylinder car; in a short time, we would get another report, that the car taken from James was found abandoned somewhere, and someone else would report the theft of a car more to the liking of Clyde Barrow.

In the meantime, newspapermen in Dallas swarmed all over Sheriff Schmid. Why had he been so reluctant to ask for help from the Dallas city police department? How could he have had Clyde Barrow in his gunsights and allowed him to get away? Why hadn't he ordered his men to shoot on sight, rather than allow the Barrow car to fire first and to pick up speed to make a more difficult target of the killers who were blamed in six or eight murders already? And on and on.

The trouble with questions like those is that there were no answers that could be given that would be politically wise in the least. Smoot merely said all of us had missed a good chance, because we waited to make certain they would not give up when he had ordered them to stop.

"It wasn't a total failure," Smoot said. "At least we didn't get any of my men killed like they did up in Missouri."

It wasn't enough to satisfy the newspapermen. So Smoot said he had a surprise for them: actually, he said, the sheriff's department has one of the Barrow Gang in custody; at this very minute, he said, his deputies were running down more leads offered by this young tiger named W. D. Jones, who claimed Clyde Barrow held him against his will. And if the newspapermen would like to have a *real* story — better than the one they were planning to write — why didn't they step inside his office and see a twenty-eight-page statement W. D. Jones had signed?

Alcorn winked at me. The wink meant that Smoot could handle the situation nicely. He also said he had talked to Smoot earlier in the day and told him he'd like to have Ted Hinton as his full-time partner.

What we would do, Alcorn said, was get ourselves assigned to only one mission: to bring in Clyde Barrow and Bonnie Parker, dead or alive.

And, he said, after the newspapers were through roasting the sheriff for missing his chance to put Clyde and Bonnie away for good, he'd probably be receptive to the idea.

DALLAS PUBLIC LIBRARY, HAYES COLLECTION

LEFT TO RIGHT, SHERIFF SMOOT SCHMID AND DEPUTIES ED CASTER, TED HINTON, AND BOB ALCORN RECOVERED THESE ARTICLES FROM THE CAR BONNIE AND CLYDE ABANDONED AFTER THE NOVEMBER 23, 1933, SHOOTOUT AT SOWERS.

XII

Full Time on a Hard Trail

SINCE THE incident at Sowers, and after looking at the slight effect the Thompson submachine gun had on the steel body of Clyde's V-8 in that exchange of shots, I discarded the tommygun for good. Hatton Sumners was our congressman in those days, and he was down for the Thanksgiving holiday, so I went to see him. What I wanted, which I was certain he would arrange for me, was a Browning Automatic Rifle. I happened to know that the National Guard had stacks of them and ammunition that was going to waste. And, revealing it for the first time to anyone, I told him Smoot had assigned me full time with Bob Alcorn to hunt down Clyde and Bonnie and bring them back dead or alive.

The big miss at Sowers, and the heat he was taking in the newspapers for not firing first and asking questions later and for not letting the city police officers and even the Texas Rangers in on the ambush, had changed Smoot's attitude completely. The newspapers presumed he had a sure tip that Clyde Barrow and Bonnie Parker would be where they were; the fact is, we had no such tip. We only had a hunch, based on the way Clyde's mother, Cumie Barrow, had appeared to me when I saw her, that she would be meeting with her son *somewhere*. It was only a wild guess, and it was another guess that they

111

might meet out near the dairy farm on the right-of-way of State Highway 15. To have alerted half the state of Texas because I had a hunch something would be happening would have been laughable. Every encounter we had had with Clyde up to this time was simply luck; it would prove that way in the future, and, more times than not, our luck would turn sour.

The congressman made a telephone call and that was all it took to get me a B.A.R. like Alcorn's and like the one Clyde Barrow used with such deadly effectiveness in tight spots at Joplin, Missouri, and Dexter, Iowa. I loaded the back seat of my car with ammunition, so I could get in some practice rounds in a few out-of-the-way places in the Trinity River bottoms.

My skinny friend Preacher Hays would go with me — though he insisted all along that he wanted no part of guns and had signed on with the sheriff's office to serve summonses and perhaps to politick, but certainly not to kill people. "I am," Preacher said, "a lover, not a fighter."

We went out a time or two. Preacher really did have trouble holding the B.A.R., and really wasn't all that interested in staying with it. But no finer man ever lived. Anyone who has ever fired that weapon knows that it will take off and you'll find yourself firing straight up if you're not holding on tight to a B.A.R. But twice was enough for Preach.

I had trouble getting him to go with me on one errand when I was hot under the collar. Out in the Bog, which was the name they gave to West Dallas in those days, the word was out that Clyde was popping off about me, and some friends of his had heard it. I had it from several sources that he had told all his acquaintances that "Ted Hinton would be afraid to meet me face to face without bringing people with him."

I knew that Clyde knew better than that. And, hearing it from two or three people who had heard it from other people, I was infuriated.

"Get in," I told Preach one morning when I drove up alongside him outside the sheriff's office. "Where are you going?" he asked. "It doesn't matter," I told him, and when he got into the car I headed it out toward Henry Barrow's station in West Dallas.

"Wait just a damned minute," Preach said when I was still a block from where I was going. "I don't want any part of this."

"Then get out," I said, stopping the car. He was my friend; he knew me. But he knew I meant it. He was either with me or against me.

"Go ahead," he said. "I'm with you."

Henry came out to greet me.

"Mr. Barrow," I said, "I've got something I want you to pass on to Clyde, and I've brought a witness here. This is Preacher Hays."

Preacher was embarrassed because I was coming on strong. "Leave me out of this. Man, I don't want any trouble," Preach said. "You go ahead, you two."

Henry leaned into the car, and I gave it to him:

"Henry, next time you see that son of yours, tell him for me that I'll meet him alone, any time. He can name the place. I know the stuff he's spread about me, and you've heard it, and you know it's a damned lie."

"I know, Ted," he said. "I know. I'm sorry, Ted. I can't help what the boy says."

That was the first and only time I ever felt anything personal with Clyde, as long as I'd known him. I'd made frequent visits to Henry and Cumie's place, and I considered Clyde's brother, L. C., a friend of mine. I knew Clyde as well as anyone on the side of the law did, and I didn't have to repeat to his family that anything I ever did was in the line of duty. And that no one in the world would be happier than I if Clyde and Bonnie would come in. I'd given my word that if they ever *did* decide to give up the chase, I'd guarantee their safety until they had a fair trial. And I'd even raised the point with Henry and Cumie that there was always a possibility that a jury might give Bonnie a break, and, for all I knew, maybe a good lawyer could help even Clyde beat the chair.

Henry just shook his head, and Cumie sobbed softly. Henry had been through all that with Clyde, he said, and he was sad Clyde couldn't see it his way on account of what it was doing to his mother, Cumie, particularly since they'd buried Buck, and it was breaking Mrs. Parker's heart, too.

Now, all of a sudden, I wasn't angry at anybody. I had no call to unload on Henry the way I had. Without his guns, Clyde was considered by most lawmen as just another punk. Five feet seven, a nobody who couldn't write a letter of his own. But I'd never called him a punk. That's what everybody else was calling him, and probably always had, but not me. He was on the wrong track; he had gone much too far ever to turn back now. But he had guts.

I tried to comfort Henry. He seemed so down, as though he'd lost the last friend he had outside his own family. And the sad thing was, maybe that's the way he saw it when I flew into a rage at him.

"Somebody broke your window, Henry," I said.

"Yep. Always something," he said, with his head downcast. And then I found out what had been bothering him: he knew who had broken his window with some shots in the night, and this was only the latest piece of meanness to hassle him. Henry told me who it was who'd been doing it, just because he was Barrow's dad, and just because Clyde had snubbed him once. Henry was barely hanging on to his small filling station without the extra expense of repairing vandalism and some other cowardly things designed to harass him.

I loaned Henry the shotgun from my back seat and said, "Henry, you and Preach here are the only ones who know where you got this shotgun. If you have trouble call me. But if I'm not here in time, blast his damned head off. I'll come out and make a report and tell 'em he just died."

Henry took the shotgun and the handful of shells, and he looked at them. "I'm much obliged to you, Ted. You're a decent man. I know you're out to stop my boy, and you'll probably have to kill him one day, and you're the man who can do it. But I don't hold it against you."

The old man had tears in his eyes, and he seemed to choke when he tried to get the words out. And maybe my eyes had a tear in them, too, I wouldn't know about that.

I gripped the old man's hand, started the car, and drove away, and Preacher just looked at me. "That," he said, "was two damn-fool things you did there, Ted. Three — counting getting yourself in on the job of taking Clyde and Bonnie."

Preach said he admired my guts, but right now they were growling. I had the job of taking Clyde and Bonnie, and I had no idea where they were. Through the month of December I must have had a dozen tips that they'd been "sighted" here or there, but people were getting crazy in their heads. They'd see a Ford-V-8 and a boy and girl in one, and sure as hell they'd think any stranger was Clyde and Bonnie. The sad thing was that Clyde and Bonnie scared the daylights out of people so that when someone really was held up by Clyde Barrow, two chances out of three the crime would go unreported.

Many of the reports would come far too late to be of any help at all. The office continued to get calls from peace officers who had picked up a fugitive; under arrest, the prisoner would try to curry a little favor with the officers in exchange for some wild story they could offer about the time they were with Clyde and Bonnie. They'd usually start by saying that they'd been drinking, and Clyde was drinking at the next table. And the fact was, Clyde probably never drank a pint of whiskey all told in his whole life. That was one of the reasons he was so hard to catch.

It was a rare day that these reports did not come. Some were checked out, and so Alcorn and I spent many wearisome days and nights driving from one place to another, always in hopes of finding Clyde Barrow again. Before long, we would be living in the car, seldom ever hitting a bed, just as Clyde and Bonnie were doing wherever they were.

An ex-convict named Monroe Routon was arrested in Houston on January 3, 1934, and during the police grilling he admitted he had fenced some bonds taken in a bank robbery at Shiro, Texas, on the night of February 20, 1933. Who had bought the bonds from him? He named a Kansas City politician. Who had taken part in the robbery with him? The officers took notice when he said Clyde Barrow and a younger fellow whose name escaped his memory. Was it W. D. Jones? He believed it was.

All that may have helped clear up something that happened a year before. But it wasn't much help in finding where Clyde Barrow was today.

But while we were losing sleep through the second week in January, some events were taking place without our knowing it at the time:

On January 11, James Mullen — not long out of Eastham Prison Farm near Crockett in southeast Texas — appeared at the door of Lillie McBride, where Officer Malcolm Davis had been killed by Clyde Barrow just a little more than a year before. Mullen said he'd come to find Floyd Hamilton, Lillie's brother. He carried a note from Raymond Hamilton, another brother, who had been in Eastham Prison with Mullen. There was no way for Lillie to be sure that Mullen wasn't sent by police to trap Floyd. But Lillie was convinced Mullen was all right.

On January 12, on Lillie's direction, Mullen found Floyd — who would know how to find Clyde Barrow and arrange a meeting of the three of them. On January 13, Mullen and Floyd Hamilton bought ammunition for pistols at two different pawn shops in Dallas and drove to a spot between Ferris and Lancaster, south of Dallas, where they met Clyde and Bonnie. At that meeting, plans were made to spring Raymond Hamilton from prison at Eastham Farm. It was daring in its concept. For his part in the plan, Mullen was promised a thousand dollars by Hamilton. Hamilton was certain that his pal, Clyde Barrow, would take part in the escape just for friendship. He was right.

Raymond Hamilton had been in prison since August with a string of sentences totaling something like 263 years. When he was leaving Dallas in custody of our officers, he bragged to reporters standing by, "They'll never keep me there. You know my friend Clyde Barrow won't let them keep me long. He'll help me bust out. You wait and see."

The newspapers, of course, relished having a quote like that for their front pages. And in case Lee Simmons hadn't seen the papers in his office at Huntsville, where he directed all of the state's prison system, Sheriff Schmid thought it prudent to inform him by telephone of Hamilton's boast. I remember he said, "For God's sake, watch him."

The Texas prison system in 1934 still owned about 75,000 acres of land, and roughly half of it was under cultiva-

116

tion at a dozen farms that produced corn, cotton, feed, and garden products for the prison tables. On these farms and behind the foreboding Walls at the main prison at Huntsville about 5,300 prisoners on the average were held at any given day in 1934. Escapes had reached their peak in 1929, when 302 prisoners jumped — an average of five every week. But the reforms installed by my friend Lee Simmons had cut this number to about 100 a year. Considering the number of prisoners used on work details in remote areas, the wonder is that there were not more.

It was a policy before Simmons took over as prison director to abuse the prisoners and to get conformity by the use of the bat; anyone who had a friend in the system could get prisoners for use in their cotton fields. Simmons inherited a sorry situation, but he was improving it. He still demanded a day's work out of each prisoner, but this work was in support of the prison itself and to improve conditions within the prison. He was concerned with their recreation after work and on weekends, and he set up schooling to improve the prisoner's chance of becoming an employable citizen after his sentence had been served. He was "old school" in his demands for a good day's work from every man, but he was ahead of his time in the Southwest for providing opportunities for inmates to make something of themselves through work and education. He even allowed some prisoners to form baseball teams and allowed them to take trips outside to play the town teams in neighboring communities. Prisoners staged a rodeo that, these many years later, has become a popular and colorful event attended by thousands of outsiders. His purpose was to raise morale and raise a little money for recreational equipment and library books.

But to expect that escapes would stop would be a mistake. The hatred for confinement or forced labor and the toughness of the men who were incarcerated combined to make the prison guard's life a hazardous one. These prisoners were hard men in the hardest of times.

To discourage escapes on the work details sent out each morning, Simmons adopted some procedures that would stop all but the most desperate or foolhardy.

In addition to two armed guards with each work detail of eighteen to twenty men, a ''long-arm'' or ''backup man'' on horseback would be stationed well away from the work detail. The backup man always was chosen for his marksmanship and always was armed with a high-powered Winchester rifle that could pick off any troublemakers who might overpower any guard who was near at hand.

None of the precautions worked, however, when Clyde and Bonnie decided to free their pal, Raymond Hamilton, from Eastham Farm. Clyde knew the layout; he had done some time at Eastham himself.

Mullen, of course, had relayed Raymond Hamilton's wishes through Ray's brother, Floyd, to Clyde and Bonnie. Floyd had visited at the prison with Ray on the previous Sunday and had brought the weapons — two loaded automatics — and had planted them under a culvert near the prison wood yard. Raymond Hamilton had no access to the wood yard, but he had an old West Dallas pal named Fred Yost who had that access. Yost had become a trusty, a position that allowed him to move about with a certain amount of freedom, almost like a guard. By prearrangement, Yost had smuggled the guns into the building where Hamilton and his older con pal, Joe Palmer, slept.

In the still-dark winter dawn, on the foggy Tuesday morning of January 16, 1934 — just as they had planned — Palmer and Hamilton went to work with the guns concealed in their clothing. Prisoners in the work details were not searched. This morning, a more alert guard might have noticed that something was amiss when Hamilton did not report to his regular work detail but accompanied the sixteen other men in a woodcutting detail that included tough and slender Joe Palmer.

As they had promised they would, Clyde and Mullen were waiting in weeds alongside a ravine fifty yards away from where the detail would cut wood near the road. Clyde's B.A.R. was ready. Bonnie waited in a car not far away, out of sight due to the heavy growth of wood.

Clyde and Bonnie could not have wished for a more favorable set of circumstances as they made ready to spring their West Dallas pal. As the guard Olan Bozeman brought the detail into their work area and found Hamilton in his group, he called down the long-arm man, a dedicated prison officer named Major Crowson. Crowson approached the group on horseback — breaking a rule: he was under strict orders never to bunch up with the other officers. On this morning, of all mornings, he did.

When the guards walked to greet Crowson as he approached, Palmer had his pistol aimed at Bozeman. "Stick 'em up, boys," he said. Crowson raised his rifle. Palmer and Hamilton both began firing their .45 automatics. The guard's horse reared. Major Crowson caught a bullet in the stomach and another in the head. Barrow opened up with withering rat-tat-tat fire from his B.A.R., mostly high into the air.

The machine gun fire provided all the cover that was needed as a handful of prisoners broke and ran. One guard kept firing, even as Crowson lay dying. Two others did not — a phenomenon that sometimes happens. Some men cower in the reality of gunfire aimed at them, and some men seem to continue to do their duty even in the grip of a natural fear. It is difficult to explain.

The firing of the single guard kept most of the prisoners pinned down. But Clyde and Bonnie succeeded in freeing Hamilton and Palmer, and also Henry Methvin, and, without planning to, Hilton Bybee and J. B. French, both long-termers.

The car was revved up to go. Clyde, Bonnie, and Mullen rode in the front seat; Hamilton leaped on Mullen's lap. Mullen protested that only Palmer, Hamilton, and Methvin were in on the break. But Clyde said, "Pile in!" and revved the engine for a getaway. Palmer, Bybee, and Methvin were jammed into the turtleback according to one eyewitness report at the time. And the car headed north.

The alarm was spread, but too late. Crowson, the long-arm man among the prison guards, was carried away for treatment of wounds that he attributed to Palmer. He was fatally wounded, though he hung on for a couple days before dying. The two guards who had acted cowardly were discharged almost as soon as the report came in.

The fugitives drove on backcountry roads for the most part during the rest of the day. At sundown, a witness near

Hillsboro was found who had seen a car stop and a group of men get out and throw their striped prison clothing into a creek.

A service station attendant who had heard news of the break on the radio talked animatedly about the news to customers — who turned out to be the escapees and Bonnie and Clyde.

"Are you gonna talk," asked Clyde hotly, "or are you gonna give me some gasoline?"

The attendant, reporting the incident later to officers, said he filled the customer's tank and did not ask for payment.

XIII

Near Misses

THE RAID on Eastham Prison Farm had gone exactly as planned, with one exception: Henry Bybee and J. B. French had not been part of anyone's plan, including their own. They merely saw an opportunity to make a break during the confusion and took it. Hamilton attempted to turn them back, but Clyde could see no harm in their coming along. Neither remained long with the group. Bybee was let out of the crowded car to hitch a ride and leave the fugitive band to their own devices. Very soon, he stopped a young woman and took her car at gunpoint after telling her he had just escaped prison and would tolerate no false moves. But his years in prison had dulled his brain; when he stopped at a service station, he left the keys in the ignition when he went into a toilet. The young woman drove away quickly to the next town and notified authorities. Bybee soon was picked up and returned to Huntsville, where he was placed for safekeeping in a death cell.

French — who was given a free ride out — had also gone his own way, which had been in an opposite direction. French too would shortly lose his freedom when Louisiana officers found him. Neither Bybee nor French had more than a fleeting acquaintance with Clyde and Bonnie; neither would fit into their scheme of things.

In the interest of filling in the story of Clyde and Bonnie's movements after the break — which baffled all law enforcement people at the time — it is possible to reconstruct exactly how the fugitives eluded roadblocks all over Texas.

By taking the back roads and country lanes away from the few paved highways, Clyde and Bonnie with Hamilton, Methvin, Palmer, and Mullen drove to a prearranged retreat near the Rhome community northwest of Fort Worth. Mullen was only protecting his investment: for his carrying the message from Ray Hamilton to his brother, Floyd, and for going with Clyde and Bonnie to Eastham Farm to assist with the escape, Ray was to pay him a thousand dollars as soon as he could get it together. For Clyde's part, he expected no payment for something he surely figured would be only what any good friend would do for another. At this point, in January, 1934, he considered Raymond Hamilton his friend.

At the prearranged site near Rhome, Ray's older brother, Floyd, and Clyde's younger brother, L. C., visited the reunited fugitives that same night. Mullen rode back to Dallas with them, carrying money he had obtained from Clyde to buy clothing for Ray Hamilton, Methvin, and Palmer, who still were in their prison clothes. The next day, after repairs were made to Clyde's car, the fugitives moved to Vernon, Texas, further to the west in North Texas, and Mullen joined Floyd Hamilton and John Basden and drove there from Dallas to deliver the clothes.

Very soon the trail was cold. Certainly I was having no luck finding them around Dallas. In retrospect, I believe the search continued too long in the vicinity of the prison. Alcorn and I were certain that Clyde had shot out of that area even while prison officials were first reporting the break.

There are indications that Ray already had made some plans for making "big money" and repaying his debt to Mullen. Hamilton had hoped to become a bank robber, to make a splash rather than merely make a living from frequent hijacking of small stores and service stations. And the first plan he had was for knocking over the Lancaster Bank, just south of Dallas. But now he was without even the basic tools he needed, guns and ammunition.

Clyde knew how and where to get the best. As he and his dead brother Buck had found at Enid, Oklahoma, the National Guard Armory always had powerful weapons and .45s. There was a National Guard Armory at Ranger, another of the oil boom towns of that period. It would be a simple matter to burglarize the armory and solve the gun situation for themselves and all their friends.

Ray was willing, but he had an affair of the heart that he thought he might attend to first. Not far from Vernon was Wichita Falls, where Gene O'Dare's wife was probably lonesome. O'Dare had got himself caught in some armed robbery business and had been sent down to Huntsville for fifty years. Hamilton remembered Mary O'Dare and believed she liked him. With his knack for car theft still as good as it had been before he was sent down to Eastham Prison, Hamilton stole a car and came calling on Mary O'Dare in Wichita Falls.

In the months since Hamilton had seen her, Mary had taken the name of the man she was living with. She was Mary Pitts now. But that hardly mattered to Ray — nor to Mary, as it turned out. When Hamilton found her, Mary O'Dare returned to the gang's hideout at Vernon with him.

The photographs of Mary show her to be heavily painted, but she was a girl who would rate admiring glances wherever she appeared. But Bonnie took an instant dislike to her, and Clyde had a mistrust of any woman except Bonnie. For the time being, however, any friend of Ray's could be a friend of Clyde's. It was that simple.

On February 19, Methvin, Palmer, Ray, Clyde, Bonnie, and Mary O'Dare met with Clyde and Bonnie's relatives near Greenville, not far northeast of Dallas. And then they set out for Ranger to arm themselves, courtesy of the National Guard. It must have seemed like old times for Clyde, working with Ray Hamilton again; they loaded their car with Browning Automatic Rifles, several automatic pistols, and ammunition.

Again, they did not remain long near the scene of the crime. The next day, Clyde, Ray, Bonnie, Methvin, and Palmer met Floyd Hamilton on the Dallas-Lancaster Highway. Floyd agreed to take some of the weapons for safekeeping and to meet one week from that time at a rendezvous point at

Cedar Hill, in a hilly section of southwest Dallas that was sparsely populated and overgrown with native cedars.

On February 26, Floyd Hamilton and his wife, Mildred, took Bonnie's sister, Billie Mace, her mother, Mrs. Parker, Clyde's younger brother, L. C., and Clyde's mother, Mrs. Barrow, to meet the family members who were on the run. Ray Hamilton introduced his new running mate, Mary O'Dare. As for Methvin, he seemed merely along for the ride — a pimply-faced young fugitive who was always at Clyde's command.

Apparently no one mentioned to any of the Barrow or Parker families that they had already cased the Lancaster Bank and, in less than a dozen hours, would be robbing it at the point of Ray Hamilton's gun.

Clyde was always the mastermind. He and Hamilton would knock over the bank; meanwhile, Bonnie and Mary would be waiting together in a switch car alongside the Bluebird Farm near Wilmer Hutchins, a more southerly part of Dallas County.

A short time after the robbery, Clyde and Raymond drew up alongside Bonnie and Mary, abandoning their original getaway car in case someone had bothered to take down the license number.

Though neither ailing Joe Palmer nor Methvin had taken an active role in the bank job, they joined Clyde and Ray at Bluebird Farm. Bonnie had the motor running; then Clyde moved in under the wheel, Bonnie took the center seat in front, and Methvin sat at the right front. Hamilton and Palmer jumped in the back and Mary moved to the center to make room for them.

Only then did anyone bother to count their haul: $4,433, the biggest payday yet for any job that Clyde had engaged in. With this much money, perhaps they could take it easier for a time. At least, considering the accounts given to me by members of Bonnie's family who would be filled in on it later, Clyde and Bonnie felt that way. But the taste of a large amount of cash so easily made had an intoxicating effect on Raymond Hamilton. This amount, he said, would only be the start of what he hoped to do.

It was the division of loot from the Lancaster Bank job that began the division between Clyde and Raymond. Perhaps the friendship had already been strained when Raymond introduced Mary O'Dare into the group, making it a partnership that Clyde never would accept. The slender and sickly Palmer recounted some time later what had happened:

Hamilton was watched closely by Clyde through the rear view mirror as he counted the money. Hamilton would have liked to split the money two ways (evenly between himself and Clyde) or even four ways (something over eleven hundred dollars each for himself, Clyde, Bonnie, and Mary O'Dare). But Clyde bristled; he would take one-third, Ray would take one-third, and Bonnie, who was a part of everything Clyde did, would take her third as agreed. Clyde was having no part of Mary O'Dare; he barely trusted her, and she was only excess baggage when it came to crime. Methvin, who only rode along, was not taking a share of the loot, except whatever small tip Clyde would choose to give him. And Palmer was taking nothing. Palmer was only along for the ride, happy enough to have Clyde's company and Bonnie's and the meals they bought for him. There was going to be no share for Mary O'Dare for being a passenger that Bonnie had to watch over, and that was final.

Hamilton sulked, according to the report from Palmer that came down to us later. And, thoroughly tongue lashed by Clyde, Hamilton satisfied himself by taking a few extra bills and stashing them in a pocket. Clyde pretended not to notice, to let this pass. But he did not forget. The money was split three ways, as Clyde wanted.

At the very worst, Hamilton had enough money to pay off his debt to Mullen when he next saw him. And he had his freedom, as did Palmer and Methvin. Further, he had his old crony's good-looking wife, Mary, to keep him warm. It beat the hell out of prison life.

They headed northward, into Oklahoma.

After the breakout, the old reports of sightings of Clyde and Bonnie surfaced more frequently.

In the middle of February, before the Lancaster Bank robbery on the 27th, police at Reed Springs, Missouri, had gone to a camping site near the town to check reports that a stolen car had been seen. As they approached the car, they commanded the occupants to surrender. But instead they received a furious burst of gunfire, putting their own car out of commission. The fugitives — who were described by officers as Clyde, Bonnie, and two other men who were probably convicts they had liberated from the prison farm in Texas — were reported fleeing into Arkansas.

A few days later officers at Muskogee, Oklahoma, set a trap for a gang of strangers thought to be the Barrows and the other prison escapees. Not only the law enforcement officers were involved this time, but almost a thousand National Guard troops were called in to the Cookson Hills wilds of eastern Oklahoma.

I doubt that the fugitives were in the Cookson Hills at the time of the raid, though in fact they were headed in that direction shortly afterward. In any case, all the military movement failed to yield Clyde and Bonnie.

I am reasonably certain that witnesses who were "positive" on February 24, 1934, that the robbers who had taken $7,100 from the First National Bank of Galena, Kansas, were Bonnie and Clyde were wrong in their identification. This time Bonnie was said to have been dressed in men's clothing; I doubt that Bonnie would do that. The bandits, whoever they were, had entered the bank during the previous night and had bound the bank employees as they arrived for work in the bank in the morning. This indirect method was not Clyde Barrow's style. The Kansas robbery I would discount entirely. It is entirely possible that there was a basis for the military operation against them in the Cookson Hills of Oklahoma; the incredible speed of movement of Barrow in a Ford certainly makes it plausible that the gang could have sought refuge there and at Reed Springs, Missouri, and returned to Texas in time for the rendezvous with the Barrow and Parker family members on February 19 and again on the 26th, before the Lancaster Bank robbery on the 27th.

In their flight they may have also robbed banks at Durant and Poteau, Oklahoma; local officials contend that they were identified. I cannot say with certainty that they would have done those jobs either. They would not have needed the money, though Methvin and Palmer may have urged them to pull another major robbery so they too might have some money to spend. I am certain that during the first week of March they were all in Terre Haute, Indiana, enjoying some of their ill-gotten money and feeling a freedom from capture that they never could have been certain of in Texas.

According to other information that no lawman could have known at the time, the relationship between Hamilton and Barrow was daily becoming more strained.

Once, the report goes, Clyde was napping in the back seat of the car. Methvin and Palmer had left together, leaving only Bonnie, Mary and Ray awake at the place where their car had been parked.

Clyde never would have allowed himself the pleasure of this nap without having Bonnie or Methvin, whom he trusted completely, awake and watching out for him. And he had quietly laid down a rule with Bonnie that she would never allow Mary O'Dare to leave alone from the group. So little did Clyde trust the paramour of his old sidekick, his regard for Hamilton was falling with each day.

Now that Clyde was asleep, Raymond was flirting with Bonnie and Mary at the same time.

"Bonnie," he blurted, pulling up the .45 he always kept at the ready, "why don't the three of us just take off. We could knock ol' Clyde off right here, and he wouldn't feel a thing."

Bonnie dismissed it as a joke, though she knew Raymond was half serious at least.

On another occasion, when Clyde had left Bonnie for an hour or more after what could be described as a kind of lover's spat, Mary O'Dare took Bonnie's side and consoled her: "If he did *me* like that, I'd poison him."

The relationships of hunted people are apt to become strained, and the needling between Clyde and Raymond, when they spoke, became more pointedly barbed. Raymond could always make Clyde's anger rise with references to his own intention of becoming a big bank robber while Clyde could "stick to the filling station holdups if he wants to."

127

And Clyde could always humiliate Ray by reminding anyone in the gang of an instance or two when the big bank robber showed a streak of "yellow" or cowardice.

Palmer, who was always suffering stomach upset when he traveled, and Methvin, who worshipped Clyde as a dog might worship a master, were jumpy that the rivals might let their anger get out of hand sometime and get them all caught.

On March 6, Hamilton and Mary O'Dare said their cool "so longs" to the others, and headed back to Texas in a car that Hamilton had stolen. Everyone who knew Raymond Hamilton said he could steal cars with more finesse than anyone else.

Clyde and Bonnie, too, quickly moved from their hideout in the Terre Haute area. There was, they knew, a very real possibility that Raymond and Mary together, or either of them alone, would not be above making a telephone call that could put them on the spot. Just a tip to police that they'd find Clyde and Bonnie in a certain area would have brought half the state of Indiana down on them — and Clyde and Bonnie never could prove that Ray or Mary had had anything to do with the sudden arrival of the Law.

On March 10, Clyde and Bonnie, still accompanied by Methvin and Palmer, drove into a graveyard near Lancaster, south of Dallas. By prearrangement, a telephone call to someone had set one of Clyde's old friends in West Dallas in motion. The friend picked up Bonnie's mother, Mrs. Parker, and Clyde's mother, Mrs. Barrow, and drove them to a rendezvous with the young lovers.

It was during this week in March, 1934, that I had another chance to catch Clyde Barrow and failed. I have previously mentioned the exchange of shots near Sowers in November, 1933. There were other times, unknown probably until now, when circumstances might have permitted me to stop them. But always something happened — and it usually was the simple fact that Clyde Barrow's uncanny ability to drive a car made him a hard man to catch.

There was no way to tell when Clyde would appear, but Alcorn and I knew that he tried at every opportunity to put Bonnie in touch with her mother, and Clyde seemed to have a need to cling to his own family ties, too. They took risks to make these visits, which were most often only a few minutes together along some lonely road.

Once we thought of a heavy truck that could run their car down. Bill Biggs Excavating Company in Dallas had several big trucks and allowed us the use of a four-wheel-drive gravel mover for a scheme that almost worked.

But first I had to become accustomed to the truck, to learn how to make the most of it, if our plan had any hope of success. We drove out on Industrial Boulevard in the flat bottomland that lay near the Trinity River and divided downtown Dallas from the boggy area of poor white frame houses that made up West Dallas in that day. Few people ever called it "boulevard" at that time; the thoroughfare was hard-surfaced but wide enough only for cars to pass in two lanes. We knew that Clyde frequently had used the road when he returned to Dallas.

There was nothing subtle about our plan. We hoped we could box Clyde in, so that he would be encouraged to surrender. With Alcorn parked in a car a half-mile up the road, he could sight their passing and signal to me in time for me to start the truck and drive into the Barrow car, or sideswipe it roughly, as it got to me. Or, if it happened just right, I might be able to pull directly in front of them, to leap out and draw on them, or even to fire if they would not submit to capture. In any case, Alcorn and I would have the fugitives between us on a narrow road.

On this occasion when we tried the truck, I was parked alongside the road as we had arranged. To allay suspicion of anyone who might report the stakeout, I appeared to be working on the truck's engine while keeping an eye on the car occupied by Sheriff Schmid and Alcorn down the road. Smoot was to judge any traffic following the Barrow car, and if it appeared to be too heavy to risk the gunfire that would surely result, he would blink his lights on and off a couple of times — my signal to let the Barrow car pass and await another opportunity.

It was after midnight when the sheriff's car blinked on and swiftly off. I waited for the Barrow car to come a little nearer. I closed down the hood of the truck, got into the cab, and started the engine. I was picking up speed and heading toward the car, intending to sideswipe it at the moment it drew alongside. But — as chance would have it again — the road seemed to fill with car and truck traffic behind my own truck and also following the approaching car.

The lights from Sheriff Schmid's car blinked on and off, and once more on and off, like dim pinlights in the distance. Smoot did not want to engage Clyde just at this time; there would simply be too much risk that an innocent person would be hit by a bullet in the exchange that would result. And, in the awful event that a bystander would be killed, Smoot's chances for reelection would go out the window. The electorate might excuse him if he was too cautious and allowed Clyde and Bonnie a little more time to steal and even to kill. But if one of his deputies accidentally killed a passing motorist while trying to take Clyde Barrow, the next election would be as good as lost.

I had another look at Clyde and Bonnie that night as they flashed by me, and frustration came over me that I had missed them again. Alcorn and Schmid were pursuing now, fast behind, but several cars were between them and the Barrow car. I was certain nothing would result from a chase, but I managed to turn the truck in the narrow road and rumble off after Clyde. I knew it was a futile act.

It was small consolation when Schmid assured Acorn and me that "time is on your side."

On another occasion, even before the shoot-out at Sowers, I had borrowed a Cord automobile from Ben Griffin Motor Company out on South Ervay. If anything I could find could outrun Barrow on a highway, surely this would be it, I was told. I drove it around, to become accustomed to it, and Alcorn and I would take it out after our regular day's search in my car, just to keep watch in it from various vantage points over the city. When I got too tired to stay awake, he'd move up under the wheel and let me have my nap, and in this way, taking turns, we'd pass the hours.

One starry winter night I was under the wheel of the Cord as we waited for a break on a road that gave us a commanding view of traffic at Duncanville, just south of Dallas. Some members of the Barrow family had been sighted in that area, and, under such circumstances, it was our hope that Clyde and Bonnie might be somewhere hereabouts. We had no intention of running onto Clyde and Bonnie at a meeting with their family; though Clyde may never have given us credit for having a sense of decency about us, neither Alcorn nor I would have needlessly endangered the lives of the Barrow or Parker family. And after boasting to the world that he'd never be taken alive, Clyde certainly would not surrender without shots in the presence of his mother.

Then, almost too suddenly to think about it, the car we had been waiting for approached. "That's him," said Alcorn, with excitement. "Get going after him!" It was one of the few times I remember Alcorn ever expressing excitement; generally, he was merely businesslike. I sent the Cord rolling onto the highway, leaning forward into the wheel as if to urge it to more speed. Then I jammed the car into second gear and hoped to feel that surge of power that would let me this time overtake Clyde Barrow as he had overtaken me before.

But I had shoved too hard. The linkage ripped out, and I could not get the car shifted into third gear. The old rule prevailed: you let Clyde out of your sight and you lose him.

On another occasion we borrowed a Cadillac limousine from the Adolphus Car Rental. Alcorn and I kept it between ourselves, and at his suggestion I took it out to learn its eccentricities until I felt I could confidently push it to its limits. It was in the wee hours of morning that I saw Clyde Barrow drive past me on Loop 12, out beyond White Rock Lake in east Dallas.

"That's him," I told Alcorn, and he sat upright and pulled a gun to the ready. "Get after him," he said.

I pushed down on the accelerator, and for a fleeting few seconds I believed we were gaining on him — almost to a point of getting in close enough to take a shot to slow him down. If we succeeded in doing that, we could hold our position behind him until the chase was in a sparsely populated region where the shots that would certainly be exchanged would not hurt another single soul.

But, even this time, he ran off from us. And when we called in to alert the office to pass the word that Clyde was in the vicinity again, he had vanished. It was several days later that we pieced together where he had been, and then it was too late.

I returned the Cadillac with thanks and took my own V-8 to Pappy Stewart's garage on North Harwood. Alcorn knew something of cars from his years as a mechanic before he began his law enforcement career.

He suggested that I get the cam action changed on the V-8 and the heads ground down to give it more power. This would save us time that we'd spent scheming and borrowing vehicles to give us an advantage we knew we needed if we ever were to catch Clyde Barrow in a chase.

I recognized now that the disadvantage lawmen have is that we have to be concerned with the safety of every citizen; we have to give the outlaw — even one who had killed as often as Clyde — every opportunity to surrender. And that split second of indecision had cost several lawmen their lives.

But with a car now that I was at home in, and with a B.A.R. that could match Barrow's, I honestly had lost any dread I might have had. The immediate difficulty was finding him again for that one more chance we felt we needed.

Though the newspapers reported some of the chance encounters we had with Clyde and Bonnie, most went unreported — the way we had hoped they would. The newspaper accounts invariably said we were ''acting on a tip from an underworld source'' or ''acting on a tip from a person close to the Barrow family,'' but nothing was further from the truth. On every occasion, it had merely been luck and nothing more that brought us into encounters with the fugitives. And up to now, Clyde had embarrassed us each time simply by outrunning us.

XIV

New Help for an Old Chore

POLITICAL HEAT was burning everyone in an official capacity in the state of Texas, and the brazen lawlessness of the time was cause for much pressure. Sheriff Schmid was feeling it; the manager of the prison system, Lee Simmons, was catching it; and even the governor's office was receiving criticism.

The governor's office belonged to Jim Ferguson, who had been impeached some years before and was constitutionally ineligible to hold the office. But Ferguson was a wizard when it came to convincing the farmers and many others that he was their special savior. To get around the constitutional provisions that would have eliminated him from what had been a lucrative office, old "Farmer Jim" succeeded in getting his wife, Miriam "Ma" Ferguson, elected on the promise that voters could have "two governors for the price of one."

The heat on Lee Simmons centered mostly on the daring break in January, the one that Clyde Barrow and Bonnie Parker had engineered for their pal, Raymond Hamilton. Now Hamilton was their enemy, going his own way with his girl friend, Mary O'Dare, and becoming a partner of several old cronies in bank holdups. Ray surely feared retribution from Barrow at least as much as he feared capture by lawmen, whom he had come to hold in scorn.

As the months passed and Hamilton remained at large, Simmons asked Sheriff Schmid if his office could delegate someone who would go along with Alcorn and me on our search for Barrow and Bonnie Parker. The fact that we were about the only two lawmen in the country who knew them and could recognize them certainly on sight would seem to make it highly possible that we would catch them one day — if anyone could. Simmons sorely needed to be appearing to be searching diligently for Hamilton — and he could use some of the credit if Barrow and Bonnie were captured.

Schmid told him frankly that he figured Alcorn and I would get them, with help or not. Our months on the job, our knowledge of their habits, our acquaintance with their families and associates — all this was only now giving us some hope. And though there was only the one Dallas County murder case against Bonnie and Clyde, which Schmid figured could be pinned on them on the basis of W. D. Jones's testimony, three minor robberies within the confines of Dallas County could be traced to them — the Sims Refinery office holdup, the Neuhoff Packing Company holdup, and the Grand Prairie holdup that had netted almost nothing. Schmid felt that Barrow and Parker, and a half dozen other outlaws who came out of West Dallas to become major problems, were first his responsibility as county sheriff.

Smoot was reluctant to have it widely known that Alcorn and I were in constant pursuit of Clyde and Bonnie, to the exclusion of every other endeavor. And any time someone new was added, he recognized that Alcorn and I would first have to bring the new lawmen up to date — something that would take a week or more. And then, the two of us, in a single car, could surely move with a quicker response than two sets of lawmen in two separate cars. But Smoot wanted to do Lee Simmons a favor.

He held out one request: that Simmons wouldn't draw from the Texas Ranger force. The Rangers had a history that was fascinating to newspaper reporters, and the last thing we needed now was publicity.

Simmons assured Smoot the man he had in mind wasn't a Texas Ranger, though he had been a Ranger, and that he would listen and be part of the team with Alcorn and me. Simmons said his man, Frank Hamer, had worked primarily on the Mexican border — but politics had been instrumental in his leaving the Ranger force. Hamer accepted the job. Then there was the matter of getting approval from the Governor's office, and this was obtained, for also hiring Hamer's sidekick and next-door neighbor, Manny Gault, who was then with the Highway Department.

For the record, both were entered on the prison payroll — and only a few of us, including Sheriff Schmid, Alcorn, and myself, knew of the arrangement. When Hamer and Manny Gault came to check in with us and to be briefed on what we were planning, Alcorn and I came back in to Dallas and spent a week acquainting the newest members of our team with the places Clyde and Bonnie had frequented in the past and the West Dallas neighborhood that had spawned them and a half dozen others who, even now, were residents of the Texas penitentiary system.

During this period, Clyde grew more and more bitter about Ray Hamilton. In retrospect, it seems clear that his hatred for "the Law" began to be exceeded by his determination to settle a score with his old pal. From family sources — to whom Bonnie recounted how the break occurred — we learned she had told Clyde after some time had passed about Hamilton's remark to "bump off Clyde and come with me" and Mary O'Dare's girl talk with her that if she were in Bonnie's place, she would poison Clyde. Bonnie had withheld telling Clyde about it for a time, knowing that it would only bring a deadly confrontation.

Clyde had at first sent Palmer back to Texas from their hideout in Missouri in hopes of finding Hamilton. Palmer was told only that Clyde wanted to see Ray. He made a trip to Dallas without success in finding Hamilton. When Clyde sometime later repeated his request that Palmer continue to look for Ray, the slender fugitive who owed Clyde a favor realized the real purpose Clyde had in mind: if Palmer located him, and reported his whereabouts to Clyde, Hamilton surely would become another Barrow victim. Palmer — who maintained all along that he was "too weak with stomach problems to keep up with Clyde'' — dropped out of sight for a time and shortly turned up as a running mate of Hamilton.

On March 19, Hamilton was accompanied by his brother, Floyd, and a Dallas truck driver named John Basden when he robbed the Grand Prairie bank of fifteen hundred dollars.

Flushed with success, he wrote a long and rambling letter to Dallas Assistant District Attorney Winter King to disclaim any association with Barrow.

The letter, marked with Hamilton's fingerprint as proof of authorship, was probably sent to have his break-off with Barrow made part of the record, in the event Hamilton ever was captured. But Hamilton allowed himself to berate Clyde in the letter — his way of striking back at what must have been the blistering put-down that Clyde had given him shortly before Hamilton and Mary O'Dare split with Clyde and Bonnie. It was Barrow, according to the letter, who was guilty of the senseless shootings and robberies of helpless operators of service stations. As for himself, Hamilton implied, he wouldn't stoop so low.

On March 31, while Mary O'Dare remained outside at the wheel of a car that Hamilton had stolen, Ray walked into the only bank of the quiet little Czech town of West, south of Dallas, and emerged with twelve hundred dollars. Rains at this time of year had made the back roads almost impassable. A few miles south of the town, Hamilton's car slid into a bar ditch. Mrs. Cam Gunter of Mexia, Texas, driving with her four-year-old son, stopped to offer help. Ray and Mary took a leaf from Clyde and Bonnie's notebook: they ordered Mrs. Gunter and the child at gunpoint to ''move over,'' and after loading their guns and belongings from the car that was mired, they kidnapped the young mother and child for their kindness. Driving Mrs. Gunter's car, Hamilton and Mary left their victims off at Houston early the next morning.

The radio accounts of the bank robbery at West were heard by Clyde Barrow. Straightaway, he had an idea for avenging the smart-mouthing Hamilton had done: he headed out, along with Bonnie and his new and pliable sidekick, Henry Methvin, to a lonely spot on a high hill near Grapevine. Clyde and Hamilton had used the place as a rendezvous point before after they had outrun the hated "Law." And Clyde figured Hamilton just might go there again while he cooled off and the chase for him was on.

Without knowing that Hamilton had gone to Houston instead, Clyde, Bonnie, and Henry took turns as lookouts that Easter morning, April 1, 1934.

This was a spot where, Ray had told Clyde before, he "always felt safe." This time Clyde didn't intend for Ray to be safe at all.

But as chance would have it, two state highway patrolmen on motorcycles, E. B. Wheeler and H. D. Murphy, were routinely scouring the region for any trace of the bank-robbing Hamilton. They noticed a car parked in a field that overlooked the highway, but they did not stop, at least not yet. There would be nothing particularly unusual about a car parked in a field — probably lovers passing the time on a sunny Easter morning. But when the patrolmen returned, they decided to have a look. It would be a mistake, and their last one.

Bonnie was asleep in the back seat of the parked car. Methvin and Clyde saw the motorcycles stop and saw the officers turn into the field. They could be no real match for Barrow — and Barrow knew this. But Methvin had not been a Barrow running mate long enough to understand that Clyde saw the motorcycle officers as fair game for a little fun. Barrow intended to take them for a ride and let them off somewhere in the country after letting them stew awhile as his prisoners. He had done this before, with W. D. Jones, and he always seemed to enjoy using the power that heavily armed desperadoes have over unsuspecting police who walk into their net.

"Let's *take* them," Barrow told Methvin.

Methvin took the suggestion as the signal to start shooting. A shotgun blast blew Wheeler off his cycle. When Murphy drew his gun, Clyde had no choice, he felt, but to zap him. Bonnie awoke with the shots, as both the patrolmen lay dying. Clyde and Methvin returned to the car to make a getaway — but Bonnie saw some movement as the leg of one of the dying officers twitched.

A farmer named Schieffer, hearing the gunshots, watched from a distance. His eye-witness account would serve to confuse law enforcement people later — for he could not possibly have recognized anyone positively from this distance. But he was certain of one thing: he saw a woman stand over the prostrate forms of the fallen officers and pump more bullets into them.

I was riding around that Easter Sunday morning with my wife and small son, who by now was exactly three months old, having been born on January 1, 1934. We drove directly to the scene of the shoooting, but other officers had preceded us there by several minutes. Already they had picked up the hulls from shotgun shells, the casings of some bullets fired from a B.A.R. and from a pistol. Already they were interviewing the farmer who had witnessed the shooting and were arranging for him to come down to the sheriff's office in Dallas to look at some pictures.

His identifications, which would prove embarrassing, included one of Bonnie's sister, Billie, who had an absolutely airtight means of proving she was not there but at her home in Oak Cliff in Dallas.

The farmer was equally certain that the man he saw — one of the two men he saw — was Floyd Hamilton, brother of Ray Hamilton. This was false, too. Though Ray's brother, Floyd, may have been up to no good somewhere, he was definitely nowhere near when the patrolmen Murphy and Wheeler were slain.

Even so, in a case of shameful harassment, Billie Mace was picked up and arrested.

It was Tuesday, April 3, when we set out for Oklahoma from Dallas, for the first time introducing Hamer and Gault to the chase. They followed us by way of the old Highway 77 toward Sherman. The reports we were belatedly getting from service station operators were that the fugitives had headed north — an indication they might be going into the relative safety of the mountainous blackjack-covered hideouts in eastern Oklahoma, or possibly that they already had passed through en route to Louisiana, where Henry Methvin's people lived.

According to my notes, on the afternoon of April 4 — Wednesday — we were driving through Durant in south-eastern Oklahoma, not far north of the Red River, which is the border between Texas and Oklahoma. On this pleasant week-day afternoon the streets were unusually crowded with cars and with people, for Durant was a rather busy county seat town. I was driving; Hamer and Gault were in the following car, though, as I recall, they were out of my rearview mirror vision when, suddenly, Alcorn at my side said, ''Here they come!''

Meeting us, drawing alongside, and passing us by were Clyde and Bonnie. They did not see us — at least they did not appear to recognize us. We could make a U-turn in the center of the street and perhaps pick up a pursuit after them. But the streets were filled with people. We could easily have got some shots off — just as certainly that would have alerted them that they had been recognized. Instead, I took Alcorn's signal, a shake of the head, and made no sudden move. We had our orders from Sheriff Schmid on that score: we were not, under any circumstance, to engage Clyde and Bonnie in a gunfight in any populated area. Instead, we kept driving at our normal speed, so as not to alert them. Apparently they had not recognized us. In my rearview mirror, I watched as they headed down the Main Street of Durant at their same speed.

We did, however, pull over to the side of the road, and in a short time Gault and Hamer had pulled up alongside us. We told them what we had seen. Now we would follow after them, being careful not to miss any turnoffs they might have taken, and pick up the chase for Clyde and Bonnie.

Soon we learned where the fugitives, still with Methvin as the third person in the ''gang,'' had gone. And the news again followed the death of a peace officer.

On April 5, 1934, Clyde and Bonnie and Henry Methvin were seen during the afternoon and again in the early evening in and near Texarkana, Arkansas. The woman — identified as Bonnie Parker from photographs in a detective magazine on sale in a drugstore — entered that drugstore at 1 P.M., while two men waited in an automobile outside. One of the men finally sauntered into the store, waited momentarily, and left again with the woman. She left half of a sandwich uneaten on the drugstore counter.

Some hours later, the three were reported seen buying drinks at a lunch stand five miles north of Texarkana. Still later, they were seen crossing the Index Toll Bridge ten miles north, after they had driven away from the toll gate without paying the twenty-five cents toll. A hastily set roadblock netted nothing at all.

All through the evening reports came in with enough elaboration to lend credence to theories that the fugitives had been in the Texarkana area. A woman at a lunch stand said she saw guns in the car. And at 1 A.M., April 6, an ice company employee reported he saw a car stuck in mud on a road near the city. When he stopped to offer help, one man and a woman fled to a nearby wood. Momentarily they emerged again in the clearing and climbed into a second car that had stopped for them.

In retrospect, there is no difficulty in piecing together their movement during the hours of night that remained. They were many miles north, and another man was about to die.

The rains that had followed Easter Sunday were general throughout northern Texas and Oklahoma, throwing the back-country roads into a near impassable state. So it was hardly unusual that truck driver Charles Dodson came upon a Ford V-8 near Miami, in the northeastern corner of Oklahoma; the two men and the woman with the reddish-blond hair inside the car had hailed Dodson and asked him to pull them out of the muddy, rutted road. Two other men already were trying to push the car to the drier center of the road, but they were having no success.

Dodson recounted the incident later:

"They said, 'If you don't get a move on, we'd as soon shoot you as to look at you,' and I believed them. I noticed a bullet hole in their windshield, and a man who was passing by at the same time must have noticed that hole, too. And he heard the threat they made to me."

The man who overheard the threat went immediately into Miami and reported what he had seen to Chief of Police Percy Boyd and to Constable Cal Campbell, who was almost twice Boyd's age, at 63. The two officers went out to investigate; the report of the "bullet hole in the windshield" brought them, though a report of any pair of young men traveling with a small blond woman might have been reason enough. There had been a general alert out for Clyde and Bonnie, and the second man (Methvin), whose identity was seldom publicized. Though Raymond Hamilton long since had broken from the Barrows, newspaper accounts invariably still linked them; people who had seen photographs of Clyde and Bonnie and Raymond still would swear those were the three people they saw.

With help from Dodson and his truck, the Barrow car was out of the mud hole and ready to roll. Dodson had returned to his truck, after regaining the chain he had used to pull the car onto the dry part of the road, when the officers approached. Dodson related afterward:

"Those in the car started the shooting; they must have fired fifteen or twenty shots. The officers fired only three or four times. Campbell fell in just about the first burst of fire from two machine guns [B.A.R.'s] and Boyd was ordered to drop his pistol after he had been hit. Blood was streaming from his head.

"They ordered Chief Boyd to get into their car. He got in and they headed out fast, over the Stepp's Ford bridge across the Neosho west and north."

Campbell had been struck by only one bullet; it had pierced his heart. His revolver was beside him on the bloody, muddy road. He had fired three bullets before he died.

Clyde and Bonnie, with their sidekick Methvin and their kidnap victim Percy Boyd, became mired again after they had sped only three miles westward from the spot where they had murdered Constable Campbell. A farmer named A. N. Butterfield approached in his car and found two men with guns trained on him. "Pull us out," they ordered. "We've just killed two men."

When Butterfield had pulled the mired car out and had been allowed to proceed on his way, he reported the incident. He did not, he said, see Police Chief Boyd in the car — if Boyd was in the car at all. That led to some speculation that the hostage might already have been shot to death and thrown out of the bandit car.

Sheriff Dee Watters said he was acting without any doubt at all of the identities of the two men and the red-blond young woman who had killed Constable Campbell and had taken Chief Boyd for the ride. Watters said he had ''been expecting'' Clyde and Bonnie since he had heard the news of the Easter Sunday slaying of the two Texas officers north of Dallas at Grapevine; Watters knew that the notorious Clyde and Bonnie had come into Ottawa County on occasion to ''cool off'' in a region that Bonnie had known as a girl.

There was only a ten-mile drive toward Chetopa, Kansas, with Watters's posse in pursuit. But Watters called it off after a time, knowing he had been outrun. There was hope, of course, that the many roadblocks being ordered by sheriff and police departments all over southern Kansas and northeastern Oklahoma might succeed in spotting the bandit car — though there would be little that any lawman could do without sacrificing the life of the officer Clyde and Bonnie held hostage.

A rural mail carrier named J. E. Allen saw the V-8 at about 1:30 P.M., just south of Chetopa, Kansas. Allen said he was certain in his mind that the car was the one he had been told about, the one that was occupied by the bandits who had killed the constable near Miami, Oklahoma, and had kidnapped the police chief who had been wounded in the gunfight.

But, wisely, the mail carrier returned to Chetopa for reinforcements. When he returned, retracing his route, he followed the car tire tracks to a point where the bandit car apparently had turned westward toward Coffeyville, Kansas.

Through the rest of the day and most of the night, lawmen from points all over Oklahoma, Arkansas, and Kansas were driving into the region where the three states converge; they were working without sleep, just as Bob Alcorn and I and Hamer and Gault were. Our team was in the best possible position to take the fugitives if we were lucky enough to come upon them. I would say we were better armed than the other officers. We were in two cars, my own and the one Gault was driving behind us, so in a fire fight, if it came, we would have the extra mobility. And, alone among the officers on the chase, Alcorn and I could readily spot them.

By dawn, as we were returning to the sheriff's office in Coffeyville to await any news that might be telephoned in, word came that Barrow had released his hostage, Percy Boyd, near Fort Scott, Kansas. In a short time, we were hearing the story direct from him:

"They have no fear of being captured," Boyd said. "They think they're much too smart for that to happen. They said they were truly sorry they had to shoot Campbell, but they kept joking about it all of the time they held me.

"Barrow and Bonnie sat in the front seat and I sat in the back with the other man. We drove to Chetopa, Kansas, and then turned north through Bartlett, the only town of any size we passed through.

"During the day we stopped three times for gasoline. None of the filling station attendants seemed to suspect they were filling up Clyde Barrow's gas tank. In our traveling, mostly we used the byroads, and rarely got on a main highway."

Boyd said he talked quite a bit with Bonnie. "She said she didn't want her public to think of her as a girl who smoked cigars, because nice girls don't smoke cigars. She was pretty mad about it."

Boyd had seen the photograph, the retouched picture that had been widely printed. Through his ordeal of capture — with the threat of dying ever-present — Boyd stood firm; he is the type of man who would be firm, I thought when I talked to him. He bore the bloodied aftereffects of the shot that grazed his scalp. And, much later, in discussing Boyd with members of his family, Clyde remarked that Boyd was "a brave man" — and this was the reason he wasn't killed.

The officer said Barrow carried a regular arsenal; he counted two sawed-off shotguns, a number of pistols, and three machine guns (B.A.R.'s). They had traveled through much of the afternoons on side roads between Pittsburg and Fort Scott; they had driven into Fort Scott late in the afternoon and purchased a newspaper that carried preliminary accounts of the slaying of Constable Campbell and the abduction of Police Chief Boyd.

"That was the first time I knew, for certain, that Campbell had died," said Boyd.

They had bought food, along with the newspaper, and had taken the food with them as they drove to a wooded area out in the country and ate together while they joked. Boyd said he was surprised that "no one seemed to be looking for us, and no one seemed to recognize any of us. I would have thought they'd have at least recognized Clyde and Bonnie. But I suppose the people who aren't in law enforcement don't notice the faces of the criminals they see in the papers as much as we do."

We didn't know much about Henry Methvin, and we wanted to hear as much about him as Boyd could tell us. At the moment, at least, Methvin's face was pimply, as though he had some kind of skin infection. "He's a lot like Barrow," Boyd said. "Cocky. But it's easy to see that Barrow is the kingpin. The others depend on him and do what he wants."

Barrow took pains to deny that he and Bonnie had anything to do with the slaying of two officers at Grapevine recently. Boyd may have bought that story, but Alcorn and I knew that old hound wouldn't hunt. Blaming someone else for it would only wind up causing trouble for people he had no intention of hurting.

Boyd said they had returned to Fort Scott during the night to search for a car they could steal, but Barrow couldn't find one to suit his taste, so they left again. It was almost dawn when they released Boyd near a farmhouse. They took some chances doing that — for they must have known Boyd would get to a telephone as soon as he could and alert the world that Barrow was in the vicinity of Fort Scott. And that is what he did.

XV

The Hamilton Split

DAYS RAN into weeks away from home while we pursued each lead we could get. Always we seemed to arrive just behind the departure of Clyde and Bonnie and Henry Methvin from any given area.

We had scoured the swamps in the Louisiana back country and the smoky hills of Arkansas. We came to know each place in northeastern Oklahoma, where Bonnie had spent some time when she was growing up and where she had friends and relatives. We had met with local law enforcement people, generally no more than one or two good men in each area, and shared our experiences with them. And generally we got their assurances that Clyde and Bonnie, who had taken the lives of so many law enforcement people, would receive high priority in their individual areas. Gradually, we felt, the area in which the fugitives could go without attracting attention was shrinking.

But each time we seemed to have placed them in a definite area, reports would come of crimes committed at some distant point outside the area where they were last seen. A bank robbery in Kansas once sent us swinging into that state — when we were near certain they were in Louisiana.

If we were accomplishing anything — and most of the time it was difficult to convince ourselves that we were — it was that we were keeping them on the run.

We told ourselves that if their physical resources were being drained as ours were, living in our car for the most part and taking sandwiches along for snacks as we searched, then we could be reasonably sure that they would make a fatal mistake somewhere.

As we searched, some action was going on back in Texas to shut off the assistance that was being given the fugitives by friends and relatives. Both Clyde and Bonnie seemed to have a compulsion to visit their mothers, despite all risks involved in arranging and carrying out the secret meetings without being detected.

They had, as a Mother's Day present, carried a white bunny around for weeks in their car, awaiting an opportunity to get near Dallas to deliver the rabbit to someone who would carry it on over to Mrs. Parker. That rabbit, delivered after Easter but before Mother's Day, represented the young couple's daring. With all of the Southwest on the lookout for them, it may seem incredible that they'd worry about the delivery of a white rabbit to Bonnie's mother. But, in fact, they got away with it.

The Texas Rangers and other law enforcement officers set about systematically to arrest family members and friends of Clyde and Bonnie. The roundup of some known associates of the outlaws would obviously be, under today's laws, a violation of their civil rights. In those days the practice was not uncommon — to take someone to jail or otherwise hold them without clear charges. The arrest ledger would merely be marked ''For Investigation.''

The practice was so common that even the newspapers reported without expressing any shock that law enforcement officials had ''declined to say where the persons arrested were being held — to prevent lawyers from finding them and setting them free again.''

It was on one such order that James Mullen was arrested at his South Dallas home, though there was at this time no knowledge of his part as the go-between who had helped arrange the raid on Eastham Prison Farm when Clyde and Bonnie sprung Raymond Hamilton, Joe Palmer, Methvin, Bybee, and French. But after the arrest and search of Mullen's house, there was a reason to hold him: among his effects was a .45 pistol that was traced to the National Guard Armory at Ranger.

Even Mrs. Barrow was whisked away for questioning. She returned to her home sometime later, expressing no hard feelings that she had been picked up without charges. She said at the time that she "hoped Clyde and Bonnie wouldn't risk themselves to pay me a visit on Mother's Day." In fact, they already had apparently paid their Mother's Day call in advance and delivered the white rabbit.

Billie Mace — Bonnie's sister — and Raymond's older brother, Floyd Hamilton, were arrested and charged with the murders of Highway Patrolmen Wheeler and Murphy. I couldn't believe it at the time. Fingerprints found at the scene were Clyde's. There was no real connection between Floyd Hamilton and Billie; they had been in school together, some-one said, when they were children.

The case against Billie Mace and Floyd Hamilton rested solely on the identification made by farmer William Schieffer, who had seen two men and a young woman at the scene of the Easter Sunday killings at around ten in the morning and again when he passed with a load of rock in the early afternoon when the shootings occurred. This was enough to get indictments and win some reward money for the officers who arrested Billie and Floyd, even as they were protesting their innocence and had iron-clad alibis: they could prove they weren't anywhere near the scene at the time!

After a time, Floyd Hamilton would also be charged in aiding the escape at Eastham Prison Farm — based on the fact that he had visited his brother shortly before the break. Though the several arrests had brought charges against Mullen and Floyd Hamilton — which could be justified — the jailing of others merely for being related to fugitives didn't set at all well with me. I counted myself fortunate that I didn't have to take part in the arrests, having been placed exclusively on the search for Bonnie and Clyde, who were carrying Henry Methvin along.

While all this was happening, Raymond Hamilton and Mary O'Dare avoided the Dallas area. They took a trip to New

Orleans, where they apparently began to worry that they would soon be blamed for the killing of Wheeler and Murphy — probably as soon as the alibis of Billie Mace and brother Floyd Hamilton were checked out. Some newspaper stories had, in fact, speculated that they had probably been "cooling off" at Grapevine after the bank robbery at West just the day before when they were "surprised" by the two officers.

Law enforcement officials in Dallas became aware of the New Orleans trip when a letter from Hamilton arrived at the office of a lawyer in Dallas. Written on Lafayette Hotel stationery, and bearing a fingerprint that was determined to be Raymond Hamilton's, the letter disclaimed any present association with Clyde and Bonnie. Clyde, according to Hamilton's letter, was "too fast for me."

Sheriff Schmid dispatched another of his deputies to New Orleans to follow the lead from the Lafayette Hotel, where Ray and Mary O'Dare had made an impression as a well-dressed couple and also as a pushy pair who had jumped in front of another couple to get a taxi to the depot. The deputy brought back word that they had probably caught a train for Chicago.

But a few days later, about April 20, Mary O'Dare was reported living in Amarillo. Lawmen took a neighboring apartment and watched for any sight of Hamilton but found none. Then, quietly, on April 23 they moved in on Mary O'Dare with the hope of convincing her that her part in the West bank robbery could be proved — but she could become a witness against Hamilton and lighten her own punishment. To further encourage her to waver in her loyalty to Hamilton, she was held quietly at the Cadillac Hotel in Amarillo, charged with the bank robbery at West.

At the time, her plea was that she "didn't love Ray" and "I only went with him because he promised to buy me nice things." Further, she said, she really intended to go back to the tailor Barney Pitts at Wichita Falls.

In the meantime, though we were not aware of it until a short while later, Hamilton had spent all his money and was reduced to riding freight trains. And, realizing that he would lose his girl friend if he couldn't come up with some money, Hamilton thought he saw his duty: to rob another bank.

With a young man who had no experience in such affairs — a boy named T. R. Brooks, whom Hamilton had met on one of his freight train rides — Hamilton stole a car and on April 25, 1934, held up the First National Bank of Lewisville, just north of Dallas. From the beginning, even as Hamilton and Brooks fled northward with six hundred dollars to spend when they reached Oklahoma and made their way back to Mary O'Dare in Amarillo, Hamilton surely knew that the affair had been botched. Police cars seemed to lurk all along the way toward Sherman.

There was the matter of radios, only now coming into general use to help in law enforcement in the Southwest; radios brought out more lawmen than Hamilton had seen before.

The capture of Hamilton this time was as simple as pulling a speeder to the side of the road. Confronted as he turned onto a side street in the community of Howe in Grayson County near Sherman, close to the Oklahoma border, Hamilton leaped from his car with his hands held up.

"I guess you know who you've caught," he said to the three arresting officers. "I'm Raymond Hamilton and I don't intend to give you any trouble. I'm just fresh out of ammunition, money, whiskey, and women. Let's go to jail."

Considerable excitement accompanied the news that Hamilton had been caught. Just twenty-one, Hamilton had become a name known throughout the Southwest. As he was brought into the Dallas County jail, the lobby filled with people from the street, curious to see the desperado they had read about.

When he was taken up to a heavily secured cell, he was shown a newspaper with an account of Mary O'Dare's statements about him. And he had been on his way to see her, with money from the bank robbery! He read the story and threw the paper to the floor.

"There's no such thing as a real friend any more. I only robbed the Lewisville Bank because Mary sent word she needed the money."

He was, I am told, the picture of dejection; he was sunburned, weary, and snappish. He was allowed to talk with newspaper reporters for a time, and when he finished telling his story of recent days, a pathetic story of riding freight trains and teaming up with a kid who'd never had any experience at robbing, he hung his head on his chest. Reporters were told their time was up. But as they departed, Hamilton called out to them: "Please . . . don't paint me as a bloody murderer. Remember how gently I gave up. Write it that I gave up with no trouble."

In the hours that followed, the case against Ray and his brother, Floyd, began to grow stronger. In jail at Crockett, in the county where the prison guard, Major Crowson, had been killed in the prison escape, Floyd found himself charged along with Mullen in aiding the escape. And both brothers were implicated along with Basden — another of those who had been picked up in the mass arrests of Clyde and Bonnie's friends and associates — with the March 19 bank job at Grand Prairie.

With Raymond Hamilton behind bars, it now became a matter of strategy among prosecutors who hoped to win a death conviction. With his escape from prison, his presence when Crowson was killed (whether it was he or Joe Palmer who actually pulled the trigger on the fatal shot), and the bank robberies at West, Grand Prairie, and now at Lewisville, the district attorney in Dallas believed a charge as an habitual criminal could be made to stick. And a jury could be convinced that Hamilton deserved the electric chair.

On Saturday, April 28, Mary O'Dare apparently decided to stick with Raymond after all. Freed on five thousand dollars bond after she was charged with aiding Ray in the West bank robbery, Mary now intended to leave Barney Pitts and said she hoped to marry Raymond Hamilton. Sheriff Schmid said he wouldn't allow the marriage to take place in his jail.

Mary's presence in the courtroom was Ray's support as the trial in Dallas began in the first week of May. The prosecution sought the death penalty; Hamilton's attorney tried merely to have his life spared.

When Hamilton was dressed in suit and tie, his appearance could evoke sympathy. In the minds of some people, there was no way a person so small and so young could have been guilty of all that was charged against him. All this — together with a natural aversion to ordering a death penalty even when the accused has been proved beyond a reasonable doubt to have willfully taken another's life — combined to spare Hamilton's life.

He insisted, perhaps with some truth, that he had not been guilty of murder. Technically, under the statutes, this might have been so. The shooting of Bucher — the result of an accidental discharge of Hamilton's weapon that first put Clyde Barrow on the road of no-turning-back — doubtless could have been proven accidental. The shots that killed the Oklahoma officer outside the dance hall at Atoka probably were Clyde's, not Hamilton's. And the killing of the prison guard during the escape, according to witnesses at the time, was quite likely accomplished by Joe Palmer. But these were not issues at trial when the state sought the death penalty on Texas' habitual criminal statute.

On May 12, Hamilton was saved at least temporarily from this fate when two on the twelve-man jury held against such a verdict.

But prosecutors wouldn't give up. They had cases in other counties against Hamilton in which, by law, the death penalty could be assessed. They would try him in Denton County to nail him for the Lewisville Bank robbery.

The trial moved quickly. The Denton jury assessed another 99-year sentence on top of the 263 years Hamilton already had been serving when he escaped from Eastham Farm in January. If it mattered, the total sentence now was 362 years — and there still was talk of moving him to McLennan County (Waco) so prosecutors could try once more to win a death penalty.

Instead, the case against him appeared stronger in Crockett County, where the prison guard Major Crowson was slain during the escape. Hamilton would be removed to the penitentiary, they decided, to await trial at Crockett.

The reader may wonder what reaction Clyde and Bonnie would have had to the letter from Hamilton that had been published in newspapers of that day, disclaiming his association with the bandit pair, and to Hamilton's subsequent arrest without so much as firing a shot at his captors.

Clyde surely would have been scornful of his former friend, whom he had taken the trouble to free from prison. Chances are, he would not have actually hunted down Hamilton and killed him — though he had put himself into a position to do that when he waited with Bonnie and Methvin at one of Hamilton's favorite old meeting spots near Grapevine on Easter Sunday. When Hamilton's letter was printed in the newspapers, we can be reasonably certain that Clyde saw it; he could always snatch a newspaper from a rural mailbox and generally find a story about himself or some of his old West Dallas friends and former friends in it. Crime news, together with the ups and downs of the nation's economic depression, was the staple of newspapers of that time.

Apparently Barrow's first response was to write a letter to Hamilton. Now he knew exactly where he was — in the Dallas County jail. But he may have had no idea that Sheriff Schmid would intercept the letter that chided Hamilton for getting himself captured.

The Barrow letter was dated April 27 and arrived three days later with the postmark "Memphis, Tenn." Whether Clyde and Bonnie's travels had taken them that far — which I doubt — does not lessen the validity of the letter. It could easily have been carried by a friend for mailing in a post office far from Clyde and Bonnie's position on that day. In retrospect it is also logical that Clyde would have dictated its contents to Bonnie. Bonnie's handwriting was later authenticated by several members of the family. But Clyde Barrow's name appeared at the bottom of the letter.

The reader may imagine Hamilton's emotions — from disappointment to rage — when he was shown the letter while he still was waiting his fate before three successive juries.

The letter follows:

Raymond Hamilton
505 Main Street
c/o Dallas County Jail
Dallas, Texas

Raymond, I'm very sorry to hear of your getting captured, but due to the fact that you offered no resistance, sympathy is lacking. The most I can do is hope you miss the "chair." The purpose of this letter is to remind you of all the "dirty deals" you pulled. When I came to the farm after you I thought maybe the "joint" had changed you from a boastful punk. However I learned too soon the mistake I had made. The first was your suggestion of shooting Joe Palmer in the back while he was asleep. You soon learned about how I felt about such "cat ideas." Since then I have found your reasons for wanting to do this was because Joe was on the farm with you and knew what kind of a guy you were. The next impression was when we got the road blocked on us in the Ozarks and you were too yellow to fight. You cowered on the floor-board, afraid of being shot. Now that you're in the Dallas jail, you have a tested pal, W. D. Jones. You might get a few pointers from him on how to impress the people you were an innocent, or possibly, forced companion of the ruthless Barrow gang. You might be as lucky as he was in making them believe I kept you handcuffed or tied.

When you wanted to get your sweetheart, I thought it O.K. But when you were so persistent about her going to town alone, that idea wasn't so "hot." I thought then, and truthfully believe now, that should she have gotten off without Bonnie she would have "spotted" us all.

She hails from a "rat" family, and you couldnt expect better from her.

You exposed your hole card when you stole the money from us on the Lancaster job. That's what I have my rear vision mirror for, to watch suspicious people. When I demanded a "shakedown," you offered such strange excuses for having the money on you I should have killed you then. I would have saved myself much bother and money looking for you. For after you writing that letter saying you didn't stoop so low as to rob filling stations, I have done nothing but look for you. Should I have found you, you wouldn't have had a chance to give up. You couldn't stand the rift of the outlaw life. For one reason you were too yellow, and knew you could never surrender with me, and another reason you wanted to play

"Big Shot" and sleep in hotels and ride passenger trains. You weren't intelligent enough to know that you couldn't live like a king and stay out. I don't claim to be too smart. I know that some day they will get me, but it won't be without resistance. You only carried your guns around to "show off." Or else kidnap women and children.

I guess you find where your boastful long tongue has gotten you. Maybe you can talk yourself out of the "chair." Or maybe you can write a few more letters. (Try one to the Governor — at least it will gain you some publicity.)

When you started the rumor about Bonnie wanting a cut of the loot you sure messed yourself up. I have always taken care of Bonnie and never asked any thief to help me. I hope this will serve the purpose of letting you know that you can never expect the least sympathy or assistance from me. So long. CLYDE BARROW.

There was no publication of that letter until some time had passed. Another one, received earlier by the Ford Motor Company and reputed to be from Clyde Barrow, was dated in mid-April, 1934, and postmarked in Tulsa, Oklahoma. If it is authentic, surely Bonnie wrote it, too, and as in the case of the other Barrow letters, it was signed "Clyde Barrow."

Even if this letter was only someone's prank, it may have expressed Clyde's true sentiments. Written one week after the slaying of Constable Cal Campbell at Miami, Oklahoma, a short distance northeast of Tulsa, the letter was not made public until much later. It was probably only one of many fan letters addressed to Mr. Henry Ford, the car maker. These lines were included:

Dear Sir. While I still have got breath in my lungs, I will tell you what a dandy car you make. I have drove Fords exclusively when I could get away with one. The Ford has got ever other car skinned. And even if my business hasn't been strickly legal, it don't hurt anything to tell you what a fine car you make in the V-8 . . .

The company files in Detroit note, as a kind of footnote to the history of the 1930s, that the senior Ford — probably unaware of Clyde Barrow's identity — had his secretary routinely reply with thanks and mail the reply to Barrow in care of "General Delivery, Tulsa, Oklahoma."

There is no record that Barrow ever thought to pick up his mail.

There is one additional letter, badly typed; it was received by Assistant District Attorney Winter King in Dallas. The family of Barrow rightly insisted, of course, that Clyde did not know how to type. And the family of Bonnie Parker is certain that Bonnie's education and awareness of spelling would not have permitted her to mail a letter with so many words misspelled on the original. This taunting message, which was typed on a Western Union blank and apparently mailed from McKinney, a short distance northeast of Dallas, could easily have been a hoax. The family believes it was. Nevertheless, the Dallas Bertillon office (a private firm that checked fingerprints) authenticated the fingerprint identification alongside the typed "Clyde" at the end of the message. It would not have been impossible for Clyde to find access to a typewriter — and a determined outlaw with a fifth-grade education might actually have composed the letter to make matters worse for Raymond Hamilton.

Readers may enjoy speculating on the authenticity of the letter, which was reproduced photographically in newspapers at the time. Hamilton was shown the letter after his trial in Dallas, in early May, 1934, had resulted in a hung jury. The message, with the spelling duplicated as well as possible, follows:

Mr, KIng
So Raymond Hamilton nev er killed anybody. If he can make a jury believe that I8m willing to come in and be tryed my self. Why dont you ask Ray about those two pol icemen that got killed near Grapevine? And while you are it bwetter talk it ov er with his girl friend. Bonnie and me were in missouriwhen that happened but where was Ray?coming back from the West bankjob wasn't he? Redhot too wasn8t he? I got it straight. And ask hi m about that escape at Eastham farm wherethat gard was killed. Giess he claims he

doesnt know fire any shots there don8t ge? Well if he wasnt too dum to know how tp put a clip in a automatic he'd hace fired a lot m ore shots and some of the vrest of the gards would got killed too. He wrote his lawyer he was too good for me and didnt go my pace, well it makes a me sick to see a yellow punk like that playing baby ad making a jury cry over him. If he was half as smart as me o the officers couldnt catch him either/ He stuck his fingerprint on a lett er so heres mine too just to let you k now thjis is on the leve;

X Clyde

P s AsK Ray why he was so dam jumpy to get rid of those yellow wh eels on his car and akshis girl friend how they spent easter

Some efforts were made to capitalize on the serious split between Hamilton and Barrow. Hamilton could provide help in capturing Barrow, and back in Dallas that was discussed. But there was nothing really that could be offered to Hamilton in return; the state was demanding a death sentence. If some leniency could have been arranged — perhaps a life sentence and a promise to drop efforts to send him to the chair — there is reason to believe Hamilton might have helped put Clyde on the spot.

But none of this came to pass. It was still up to us to stop Barrow. And we would have to do it the hard way.

XVI

Ambush: The Real Story

WE ROLLED in Saturday night at the Inn Hotel in Shreveport. The accommodations were neither the best nor worst of the motels, but the Inn had one feature that was especially appealing: we could park our cars under the motel and take a short flight of stairs to our rooms. The weapons, veritable arsenals that we carried, could be locked in the car, covered with a blanket in the back seat, and more weapons and ammunition were in the trunk.

Those weapons were kept shiny and ready. There was so little else to do. And we knew our job wouldn't be done until we'd used them. There was no need now to imagine any circumstance that would arise that would ever make Clyde and Bonnie give up; both had vowed to take some officers with them when they went.

But I wondered under just what circumstance the next meeting with Clyde and Bonnie would come for Alcorn and me, and now with Hamer and Gault. Henry Methvin would be with them and this would be more firepower on their side. And Joe Palmer, too, would probably be with them. Four desperate people, all facing the near certainty of the electric chair if they were ever brought in — so no one except a fool would seriously consider that they would end any other way than dead. It would be either them or us. Had they killed eleven people or was it ten, or was it more? And at least nine were peace officers.

But on this Saturday evening, nearing midnight, May 19, 1934, I carried only my pistol with me as we checked in with the night manager of the Inn Hotel, dragged ourselves up a single flight of stairs, and fell into bed.

On Sunday morning, I felt more refreshed than I had in weeks. Alcorn and I had spent several nights and days with little sleep, other than the dozing we could get while we drove. We had a plate of ham and eggs and grits in the diner — a respite from the bologna sandwiches and sardines that were our usual fare on the road. And we lounged away some of the day with a card game and writing letters home. I missed seeing my wife, and I missed my boy. He was coming on to five months old now, and I could count the days on my fingers that I'd had any chance to spend some time getting to know him. What kind of life was this?

During the early evening, we called Shreveport Police Chief Bryant. We wanted to introduce him to Gault and Hamer and to let him know we were in town again. He suggested we come on down to his office, to meet him there. He had ''a funny thing'' to tell us about.

This is the story Bryant related to us:

Two of his Shreveport officers had driven past the Majestic Cafe, cruising slowly. (This had to have been about the time we were checking in to the Inn Hotel.) Without any prior knowledge that Clyde and Bonnie were parked outside the Majestic, the cruising police car had inadvertently jumped them. Believing they had been seen, Clyde and Bonnie blasted out of their parking space and sped away. It was only then that Bryant's men noticed them, and pursuit was quickly abandoned.

The most interesting part of the story was what was happening inside the restaurant at that time: a young man was waiting for a stack of sandwiches and soft drinks ''to go.'' When the young man noticed the car outside hurry away, he got up and left without even a fare-thee-well, without his sandwiches, and without paying for them.

I glanced at Alcorn and nodded. "Henry Methvin," he said.

Bryant said he wasn't certain, but that had entered his mind. The waitress who had taken the order had told him she didn't know the man, never saw him before in her life. But she swore she would know him the next time he came in.

On Monday morning, we took our breakfast at the Majestic and learned from the manager the name of the lady who had waited on the fellow who had walked out. She agreed to come down to talk to us, even though she was not due to come in until the evening shift.

I handed her a sheaf of photographs. "See anybody in there who looks like the man who wouldn't wait for his sandwiches?"

She picked out the picture of Henry Methvin straightaway. "That's him," she said. "Same eyes, same pimply face. There's no mistake."

Our next move was to recognize what Clyde and Bonnie would do in such a situation. With Henry afoot and out of touch, they'd make an effort to get back together again. They'd circle back to Irvin Methvin's place, near Mount Lebanon, south of Gibsland, and Old Man Methvin soon would be hearing from Henry down there.

Alcorn and I had spent some miserable time down there already, avoiding direct contact with the senior Methvin but learning the region in what is called the Black Lake area over in Bienville Parish.

Methvin's father lived off in a forest southwest of Mount Lebanon. It's in a region where the swampland rises up in soaring ridges of pine stands and deep underbrush. In May, there would be timid flowerings of spring around a pleasant old white church that pioneers had founded there in 1837, and I remember a great red barn in a picturesque setting. Around the countryside the modest farmhouses with their gingerbread carvings and front porches reflect a kind of down-to-earth hominess. The rural folk seated on the porches always waved at passersby.

But we were always careful to make only a few people aware that we were what they would call the Law. Word

HENRY METHVIN

spreads quickly; if a neighbor learned that anyone had been around inquiring about Old Man Methvin's boy and Bonnie and Clyde, someone would straightaway let the old man know. And any hope we might have of springing a trap on them in this area would vanish.

We had managed to learn of the senior Methvin's habits, where he lived and the roads he used in his comings and goings. His Model A truck was something of a one-of-a-kind in the area in that day and time.

When Alcorn and I went alone in my car without any markings, it gave no idea that we were law enforcement officers. Alcorn and I would pass jokes that we'd come a whole lot nearer being mistaken for tramps than sheriff deputies assigned to catch two of the nation's most wanted fugitives.

In this region where the Methvins lived, farmers eked out a bare living from cotton grown in the clearings. As in so many other places we'd been since we took up the pursuit of Clyde and Bonnie, a lot of the people were barely getting by. They were living in hope that the Depression would ease up, that cotton would go up, and that by some magic there was a better life awaiting somewhere as soon as they could pick the cotton and get the money to go there. These were hard times, and they bred a generation of hard-living men. Some of the young men, like Methvin's son, Henry, left home and got themselves into trouble, and then they kept running.

Lawmen from the ''outside'' could expect no help from residents hereabouts in trapping Henry Methvin, even if he was running with the notorious Clyde and Bonnie. It was the same kind of loyalty the poor people in ''the Bog'' of West Dallas had for neighbors and kinfolk. When we ran into Clyde and Bonnie, it would probably be merely by chance, and then we'd take our chances that we could get the drop on them.

One man who would know the swampy, tree-covered Black Lake area of Louisiana best would be Sheriff Henderson Jordan of Bienville Parish at the courthouse in Arcadia. It was common courtesy to let him know we were coming back to his territory again, and he would do anything we asked.

Arcadia is about fifty miles east on U.S. 80 from Shreveport. We passed through Minden on our way to see Sheriff

Jordan and made our way through some road construction, turning onto a detour around a bridge and moving slowly. Like waking up to a dream, I saw a tan V-8, and it was Clyde, wearing dark glasses, and Bonnie at his side. They were behind me before I could react and before Alcorn could react, but he had noticed them. We had told ourselves before to remain calm so that we wouldn't make a rash move that would let them know we had seen them. In my rearview mirror I saw that Hamer and Gault did not react either, but they did not know the fugitives.

Our plan to set up an ambush near Methvin's place still appeared to be sound; Methvin was not with them, we could be sure of that.

We passed on through Gibsland, where we would return to make the run down to Mount Lebanon as soon as we could get with Sheriff Jordan and tell him our plan. Arcadia, the parish seat where Jordan headquartered, is a sleepy trading center of about three thousand people serving the farm and lumbering region around it. It was already late afternoon when we saw Sheriff Jordan and told him what we had heard and seen — and of our intention to stake out the most likely road leading down to Irvin Methvin's place. Jordan knew the country like the back of his hand; he could recognize Methvin on sight and knew all about him.

It was settled between us where we would meet; he would get his deputy, Prentis M. Oakley, and join us there a little later. We had a good and hurried evening meal, ordered a supply of sandwiches, filled a water can with ice water, and headed back toward Gibsland. There we turned south on what the natives call the ''Big Road'' through Mount Lebanon, taking the right turn at the Y southwest toward Sailes. This was the only graveled road that would lead out to Methvin's place.

We were about eight miles southwest from Gibsland when I pulled off the road and into a covering of trees. Hamer pulled up alongside in his car. There was no way we would be seen here by the passing traffic. Moss-covered trees grew so close to the road at this point that we were hidden from view — but we could see anyone approaching for almost a half mile on the road from either direction, which appeared to me to be generally east and west at this point. Our position was on the south side of the road, on a high point in underbrush that commanded a view of the road as it inclined upward at about twenty degrees on either side of us.

We settled in at about 9 P.M. Monday for an all-night vigil and came to know the night sounds of a dank forest, the strange noises of birds and animals, the creaking of tree limbs, and wind moaning through the underbrush. We crouched on the damp ground, keeping silent most of the time; when we spoke at all, we kept our voices low.

"Don't make a sudden move," Alcorn whispered hoarsely to no one in particular. "There's a snake."

There was a movement behind us as Sheriff Jordan and Deputy Oakley joined us. They had cut their lights before turning off into the underbrush, and now there were six of us waiting.

It became a tedious and uncomfortable time. Seldom have I ever been in such a nest of vindictive mosquitoes; they attacked the ears and neck and even the nose and mouth. They made the night pass slowly. The night was broken up only once, when the dim light of a truck approached in the distance. We pulled our guns up to the ready and waited as it moved closer and closer still.

"That's not Methvin's truck," Alcorn said. Two Negro men were riding in it, but they were unaware that their late night drive was being watched.

The most useful thing we knew about Old Man Methvin was the A-Model Ford truck he owned. Old trucks like his develop personalities all their own through hard wear around a hardscrabble farm. They're used like pack mules, and each comes to have its own distinctive sound. I had heard it and thought I could identify it in the dark.

But we settled back, out of sight again, welcoming the respite from the dreary and monotonous waiting among the insects.

Daylight comes slowly in the forest. In the dim light we allowed ourselves the luxury of stretching ourselves as we discussed in low tones the misery of the night, the possibility that somehow Clyde and Bonnie already had come this way and picked up Henry Methvin at the old man's place and that we might be reading about him in Kansas again somewhere. Even so, this was our best shot for the moment. If Clyde hadn't come to Methvin's place just yet, he'd be coming. And this was the way he'd come.

We ate some sandwiches we had brought in brown paper bags and continued our lookout through the day. There was time for us to doze, two at a time, in the cars that were just a little ways back in the underbrush. If a car topped the hill a half mile to the west or approached from the east, the catnappers could be alerted and into position before the car got to us.

No one really slept. Occasionally a log truck would appear; we would alert ourselves and have our guns at the ready. We would look, especially, for a tan V-8 Ford; it was a tan V-8 that Police Chief Bryant in Shreveport told us about when he recounted the story of his men accidentally jumping them outside the Majestic Cafe on Saturday night, and the same car they were driving Monday afternoon when we met them on a detour bypass at the bridge near Minden.

They would have merely outrun us; we'd have left some people killed if we had fired some parting shots at them, and they'd have been long gone.

I had a feeling, which I am certain was shared by my friend Bob Alcorn and by Hamer and Gault, who now had been with us for the better part of two months, that the fugitives would appear any minute now on this road. We would take our stance, get them into our gunsights as they approached, and at the proper time, one or two of us would rise up and give them an opportunity to "Halt."

In our hearts, no one had the slightest idea they would heed the command, but it would be given nonetheless. Always before, they had an intuitive sense of lurking danger. And always in the past, Clyde managed to shoot first or return deadly fire in the bat of an eye.

By nightfall, our eyes were red rimmed and our lids were heavy. We were dirty and unshaven; the night and day in the underbrush had left every exposed part of our face and arms crimson with smeared blood from the niggling bugs.

164

The second night seemed even longer than the previous one. We remained in a row, on the south side of the road that was running east and west. I would be first in line if Clyde and Bonnie approached from the east — and there was a reason for this: I would, we all expected, be the first to recognize them, since I had known Clyde and Bonnie. And I had a powerful Browning Automatic Rifle, the one with longest range and twenty automatic shots that would go in one side of the car and out the other. Alcorn would be second in line, Oakley third, Jordan fourth, Gault fifth, and Hamer was at the rear of the line.

However, if Clyde should approach from the west, which we had judged to be the least likely, I would have been last in line. The road was wide enough for cars to pass with ease, and a bar ditch drained it from either side. At our position, the road had been cut through a rise in the land, leaving us slightly above the passing traffic.

Log truck traffic stopped at sundown; only a few cars had passed during the day. We had watched each one and were dead certain Clyde and Bonnie had not passed this way since we had taken our places in the brush and weeds with its mosquitoes, chiggers, ticks, and lice. The night with its miseries passed slowly; I glanced at my pocket watch and it was 4:17 A.M. I passed the word to Alcorn, for no particular reason. And we settled back to wait some more.

In a short time, the silence was punctuated by the slight cough of a Model A Ford truck in the distance; as certain as the sounds of birds and animals in a swampland can be identified, the truck noise brought us to attention. We could be reasonably sure if a Model A Ford truck appeared here, it would be Irvin Methvin's. We had anticipated that Methvin's father might be out looking for Clyde and Bonnie to carry them a message concerning his son's whereabouts.

We would stop him and see what he would tell us. It was unlikely he would be out on the road at this hour of morning unless he was on a secret errand of some kind. He was startled to see us standing there in the road, our weapons drawn.

What was he doing out? He wouldn't say. Wasn't he out looking for his son? And Clyde and Bonnie, too? He insisted he didn't know anything, but he was holding out on us, and we knew it.

Henderson Jordan, the sheriff from Arcadia, said, "Mr. Methvin, we're going to have to turn that truck around, and we're going to discourage you from leaving, so you won't mind if we just kinda take you right over here easy like. We're not going to hurt you, but we'll put you right over here where you'll be safe . . . and you'll just sit quiet like."

Though the reader may have heard many versions of the senior Methvin's part in the Clyde and Bonnie story, the account that is written here is precisely what happened. When you've completed this chapter, you will understand how, for more than forty years, the stories related to Methvin's role had their beginning.

The truth is, Methvin protested stoutly and to no avail. He was handcuffed to a tree some distance behind our position alongside the road where we still waited, hoping to encounter Clyde and Bonnie. His arms were extended and his wrists snapped together with handcuffs, so that he embraced the slender tree. The position was not quite so uncomfortable as it might appear. He could stand or he could sit. But he wasn't about to go anywhere until we allowed him to go, and that was for sure.

Even by the standards of 1934, Methvin's civil rights were violated. A case might have been made under the newly enacted Lindbergh Kidnap Law, put in by the federals, that he was "kidnapped." But none of the six of us who were intent on capturing or stopping Clyde and Bonnie were thinking at that moment about whether we were justified in doing what we were doing.

Alcorn got into the truck and turned it around without turning on the lights. For our purpose, we wanted it facing east — but in the wrong lane of traffic at the side of the road. Quickly we jacked up the truck's right front wheel, which would be the one in the dead center of the road, and removed the wheel. The truck would stand as bait for Clyde, who would know in an instant this was Old Man Methvin's truck. The absence of the wheel and the jacked-up right front would cause him to slow, if not to stop completely, to offer help.

Dawn broke, and we could occasionally hear Old Man Methvin mutter obscenities at us. And occasionally, one of us — if I recall, it was one of the Louisiana officers, either Sheriff Jordan or Deputy Oakley, who lighted a cigarette for Methvin at daybreak — squatted alongside him to feed him one of the sandwiches and tried to console him.

"The FBI is going to hear about this," Methvin threatened.

"The FBI? There's no FBI here, Mr. Methvin," Hamer said.

But still there was no Clyde Barrow either. Perhaps the old man was telling the truth. Maybe he had no idea whether they'd be driving this way or not. It was 9 A.M. now, and a couple of log trucks already had slowed at the sight of Methvin's Model A truck. But seeing no one around it, they resumed their speed and passed on.

We began to discuss our situation. Two miserable nights and a full day had passed, and all of it had netted us nothing but another disappointment. The food we had brought was gone. We looked like the wrath of God — unshaven, eyes bloodshot, and feeling the wear of no sleep since Sunday. This was Wednesday, May 23, 1934.

We agreed that we'd give it another thirty minutes, until 9:30 A.M., and then we would throw the coffee on the fire and call in the dogs, to use one of Alcorn's expressions from his hunting days. Coffee? What I'd have given for a cup right then. My mouth was dry, my face was red raw; I was afraid to look at some parts of my body that seemed to be catching most of the bites from the ticks. I had a thought that on this morning in May, if I'd signed that professional baseball contract, I would only now be rising and having a breakfast steak and thinking about today's game.

If Clyde Barrow and Bonnie Parker didn't come along in the next twenty minutes, for it was 9:10, we would have missed them again. Our best hope for finding them, springing a trap on them, and getting the job over and done with, was about to flicker out. Very soon now, we'd probably have to apologize to Old Man Methvin, put his wheel back on his truck, and unsnap the handcuffs that bound him to a tree, and he'd go running off to the FBI saying we'd kidnapped him. I wondered if everyone else was dreading that as much as I was.

Perhaps it was the dread of that, and the trouble all of us might be in, that made us linger a little longer in our line alongside the gravel road in Louisiana in the eerie stillness of that morning in May.

My B.A.R. with a full clip of twenty steel-penetrating rounds in it, my shotgun — a deadly automatic with five rounds at the ready — and two .45 caliber pistols with full clips of ammo were ready for whatever happened in the next few minutes. It was 9:15.

In the distance, out of view, we heard a sound. My B.A.R. went up to my shoulder, my sights on the top of the hill where anything coming over it would appear. Call it intuition, but somehow I knew; I felt a sensation that I won't describe as eagerness, or fear, but a sensation nonetheless when your senses tell you that a gunfight is about to begin. You will shoot at another human being, and, likely, you will be shot at.

I remember the next moments so clearly, it seems I am living them right now.

All of us are concealed, but the car moving toward us is in view now, at full speed, the only way Clyde ever drove. He has caught sight of the truck and appears already to be slowing.

"This is him," I tell Alcorn. "This is it, it's Clyde," Alcorn whispers to the man spaced at the ready behind him. From the instant the tan Ford V-8 approaches, I keep Clyde squarely in my sights. I am certain the other officers are ready too.

The car has descended the hill and is approaching our position at the crest of the long and slowly rising incline. I could squeeze the trigger; I could blow the man's head off. But he is slowing; his eyes are on the truck, on the jacked-up right front of the truck in the middle of the road. He will drive in front of it, or he will come into the lane nearer to me. His eyes are still on the truck. He knows this is Methvin's truck, but he sees no one.

He has pulled even with the engine part of the parked truck, twenty feet in front of me, and he is in my gunsight, though his car is still moving. Suddenly, Alcorn's deep bellow "HALT!" arouses him. Alongside him Bonnie screams, and I fire and everyone fires, and in the awful hell and noise Clyde is reaching for a weapon, and the wheels are digging into the gravel as he makes a start to get away. My B.A.R. spits out twenty shots in an instant, and a drumbeat of shells knifes through the steel body of the car, and glass is shattering. For a fleeting instant, the car seems to melt and hang in a kind of eerie and animated suspension, trying to move forward, spitting gravel at the wheels, but unable to break through the shield of withering fire. I see a weapon go up; Clyde's head has popped backward, his face twisted at the shock of pain as the bullets strike home. No shots are firing from inside the car, but I do not notice. Now my shotgun is in my hand; the tan car seems to rock as it absorbs the blasts, but the car is moving forward, it is thirty feet away, thirty-five, it is getting away — the shotgun blasts seem to be urging the car onward. It is running out of control, down the hill now. My God, are they getting away again? Could they possibly survive all this? The shotgun has used up its automatic five shots. My ears are ringing, there is a spinning and reeling in my head from the cannonade of bullets and the clank of steel-jacketed metal tearing steel. Without thinking, I am chasing after the car, firing my first pistol until it has emptied, and I am squarely between the officers who still are firing from above me and the car that is rolling absurdly to the left and heading for the bar ditch about thirty or forty yards beyond our stakeout position among the weeds and underbrush. Alcorn is at my side now. I fire again at the sickening bloody forms inside the car and rush to the driver's side to grab the door handle where Clyde is slumped forward, the back of his head a mat of blood. There is no room to open the door; it is wedged against the embankment where the car has come to rest. With the energy that comes from who knows where I scramble over the hood of the car and throw open the door on Bonnie's side. The impression will linger with me from this instant — I see her falling out of the opened door, a beautiful and petite young girl who is soft and warm, with hair carefully fixed, and I smell a light perfume against the burned-cordite smell of gunpowder, the sweet and unreal smell of blood. I stand her up, full standing, a tiny frail girl she seems now, and I cannot believe that I do not really feel her breathing, but I look into her face and I see that she is dead. I carefully put her down in the car seat once more.

It is only an instant, a fleeting split second, and a thousand impressions are branded into my head which is searing and ringing with shots. The shots are not coming now. I reach over Bonnie to pull a pistol from Clyde's hand, and the weapon is cold. I know it has not been fired without looking at it because it has the cold feel of gunmetal, and the hand that had clutched it is still and growing stiff and slate gray against the crimson of the blood, which is everywhere.

On the floor in front of Bonnie is a pistol that is streaked with the rose color of blood. Her right hand has been shot away, and her young face is ashen gray except for the bright stain of blood from the awful blasts of shot and the reflection of pink from the flicker of sun on the red dress that is stained with blood and made a darker hue.

I straighten and see the other officers, and I know now that the job is done, and they know it, and there is time now to think it through, of all that really happened in a blazing twelve seconds at 9:15 in the morning on a lonely road south of Gibsland in Louisiana on May 23, 1934.

There was a sandwich that Bonnie had been eating; there was a Louisiana road map that was flecked with blood on the seat beside her. Clyde's B.A.R. was at his knee; he had lifted it up to the window, for it was seen there. But it was not fired. Now we could see why it was not fired. One of our bullets had struck it. He had put the larger weapon aside and had reached for a pistol to fire in one last defiant act. But he never pulled the trigger.

Clyde's tinted glasses were on the dashboard; there was no reason for him to have been wearing them this early morning, driving with the sun at his back on an early morning in May. His shoes were off. Had he been driving with only his socks on his feet? Or could he have come out of his shoes with the impact of the withering cannonade of steel bullets pounding him? I have seen this happen. The fact was, his shoes were off when I first opened the door and found Bonnie falling in my arms, a girl in red, wearing red shoes, and blood as red as lipstick painting the yellow curls in her hair.

It would not do to think long about it. Clyde Barrow — who had brought so much grief to so many people in cruel gunfire from his B.A.R., like mine — was dead. In a few minutes, the news that the young desperado — the two desperados — were dead would be flashed around the world. There would be amazement and even rejoicing about that.

I did not feel anything, least of all rejoicing. The grim job was done, the worst of it was done. There were other things that we would do, a matter of wrapping up the loose ends of a terrible chore. But the job was done. My head was ringing. I literally could not have heard thunder. The other officers, my friend Bob Alcorn, the famous Frank Hamer, his sidekick Manny Gault, and the two able Louisiana officers all reacted in their individual way, doing what we had to do. Irvin Methvin still was handcuffed to that tree. His shackles now could be unlocked, and he could be brought down to the car to have a look. His face was ashen, his lips were chalk white with anger.

He looked into the back seat of the car where a blanket covered an arsenal of weapons, clothes, and other paraphernalia. ''You've killed my boy,'' he said hotly and pitifully.

''We haven't killed your boy, Mr. Methvin. He hadn't found them yet,'' said Sheriff Jordan, with an arm on the old man's shoulder. ''Lucky they hadn't got together yet.''

Jordan threw back the blanket that covered the weapons and other gear. The old man was satisfied.

''Here's your key, Mr. Methvin. Your wheel is back on. Your truck is ready to go,'' Oakley told him. ''Sorry for the inconvenience.''

Threats were made. The old man swore he would have our hide for this. He would go to the FBI. He would tell them we had taken him against his will and handcuffed him to a tree, used him for bait.

There was time to talk, and we had Frank Hamer who could handle it. Hamer and Methvin would come to an agreement, a shaky one, and we would go along with the story that could gain currency just by not being denied: that Methvin did it for his son, to gain leniency for Henry. He set up Clyde and

Bonnie. He cooperated in some way. No one would have to say that was how it happened. People would *want* to believe that was how it happened.

What choice did the old man have? He could make trouble for us. He could indeed. But what would he want — even more than making trouble for some officers he might never see again? He'd want his son home. He certainly wouldn't want his son to die in the electric chair for his part in killing those two officers at Grapevine, Texas, when he was there on Easter Sunday with Clyde and Bonnie. He might spend some time in prison, but that was a whole lot better than dying. Hamer could make it sound logical; further, Hamer had the ear of Lee Simmons, who had the ear of the Governor.

I felt confident they'd work something out.

Oakley noticed one of the more unusual incidents of the entire affair after we had cleared the guns from the riddled death car and removed them to Sheriff Jordan's car for carrying back into Arcadia:

In the opposite direction from Clyde's easterly approach, a log truck had cleared a hill and had apparently rolled into a ditch. Smoke was rising from it, about six hundred yards from our position. I drove Oakley down there to investigate, and sure enough, the log truck had overturned. The motor still was running, and, like as not, it would have burned because it was resting there on its side in the bar ditch. We turned off the ignition.

Where was the driver? We were wondering about that when three Negro men appeared out of the woods nearby. They had topped the hill in the truck, they explained, just when the hail of bullets started. At the sound of the gunfire, when they figured all hell had broken loose, all three leaped out of the truck without bothering to hit the brakes or turn the key off. The truck kept on rolling until it ran into the ditch and against an embankment.

In years to come, that incident would gain color in the retelling, until it bore no resemblance to the actual event of simple precaution. We left the men with their truck and returned to the site of the ambush.

I made some 16 mm. motion pictures of the scene, as a friend had suggested I should if ever we came upon Clyde and Bonnie and there was time to make pictures. The movies would show how it was when it happened, so there could be no doubt, even if the landscape should change someday, exactly how it had been on this morning in May, 1934, when Clyde and Bonnie died as she had predicted they would, side by side.

We returned to the business at hand. We wouldn't move the bodies, but would leave them just as they were until a coroner jury could be called out from Gibsland or Arcadia and a wrecker could be brought to tow the car into the funeral home at the parish seat. We'd inventory the guns and try to keep visitors from messing up any fingerprints that might be around. The inventory showed, in addition to the shotgun and pistol that Bonnie had in the front seat and the unfired pistol I had removed from Clyde's hand and the bullet-damaged B.A.R. he had at his knee, three more Browning Automatic Rifles and several pistols, including one .45 caliber Colt automatic, four .45 caliber automatics, and two .38 caliber automatics.

Under the back seat we found fifteen license plates, mostly from Louisiana, Arkansas, and Texas. In the rear seat were two Gladstone traveling bags of clothing, a grocery sack of canned goods and some sandwiches, and something more than a thousand rounds of ammo, including fifty clips of automatic rifle and pistol bullets. There was some camping equipment in the trunk — and Clyde's saxophone. And there were the map, Bonnie's cosmetics, Clyde's sunglasses, a detective magazine, and Bonnie's partly eaten sandwich. Clyde had something over five hundred dollars in his wallet — we didn't bother to count it close but just noticed it.

Only a few of what would become a horde of curiosity seekers had heard the thunderous cracking of rifles and pistols — probably about 150 shots, though we hadn't yet taken count of shells expanded. The bodies of Clyde and Bonnie absorbed more than fifty bullets apiece, though some of them may have been the same bullets. We left it all as it was and kept a guard on it while we ran in and made the calls to get a wrecker and the coroner jury to make it all official. Alcorn,

CLYDE IN THE DEATH CAR

174

TED HINTON

BONNIE IN THE DEATH CAR. THIS AND THE PHOTOS ON PAGES 176 AND 177 ARE TAKEN FROM 16 MM FILM SHOT BY TED HINTON SOON AFTER THE AMBUSH.

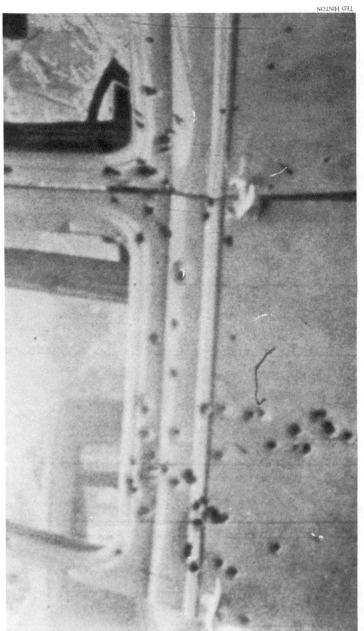

TED HINTON

THE DEATH CAR BORE 167 BULLET HOLES, ACCORDING TO A COUNT AT THE TIME.

176

TED HINTON

WITH THE BODIES OF BONNIE AND CLYDE STILL IN THE CAR, OFFICERS INVENTORIED THEIR ARSENAL OF WEAPONS.

177

Gault, and Oakley said they'd stay with the car, for the crowds were coming now. I drove in to the Texas Company Warehouse station, carrying Hamer and Sheriff Jordan with me. I put in a call to Sheriff Schmid in Dallas after Jordan had arranged for the coroner and the wrecker.

I told him what time it happened, and what it was, and he was asking questions, but I couldn't hear them. I believe he offered his thanks to me and Alcorn, but that is only a guess. I told him where we were taking the bodies; there wasn't any doubt in my mind that he'd come on up.

I indulged myself with an ice-cold bottle of soda pop, orange, to wash away the burned-gunpowder dryness from my mouth, the lingering taste of all the smells of death. Hamer called the man who had hired him, Lee Simmons, director of the Texas State Penitentiary at Huntsville. Simmons, I was certain, would get up here as soon as he could. The publicity couldn't hurt him. Hamer went ahead and dropped the hint that we'd had some great help from Henry Methvin's father. I could see a story starting that wasn't going to be at all the way it was. But my neck was one of the necks that could be saved if Hamer could get some influence used to give Henry Methvin some immunity from prosecution in Texas. Otherwise, Old Man Methvin would go to the FBI, and we could have some real heat put on us for the way we used him. We'd see what he could do.

XVII

Two True Lovers

THERE IS no explaining it, but curiosity to see a famous desperado laid out makes people crazy as loons. People came from miles around to have a look at Clyde and Bonnie all shot to pieces and to touch the car that had something like 167 holes in it, though some of the holes were probably where bullets made their exit after passing through the metal sides, through the bodies, and out the other side.

When we got back to the ambush site to meet the wrecker and the coroner jury, a great crowd was already gathered. I saw women and kids struggling along wth grown men to peek inside to get a better view of the bodies in death in the car. People were on their hands and knees gathering up the spent shell casing and digging with pocket knives to retrieve bullets embedded in trees. It was getting to be a strange kind of carnival atmosphere.

Already I was hearing men who weren't anywhere near when it was happening tell the later-arrivers exactly how it was and getting the facts all wrong. It wasn't my job to straighten it out, but I couldn't help hearing the stories.

The coroner made his report that Clyde and Bonnie died of gunshot wounds at 9:15 A.M. The men with the wrecker attached the chain to the riddled tan V-8 and pulled the car

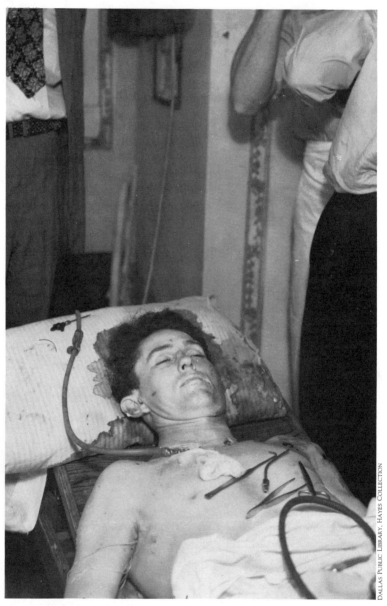

CLYDE AT THE UNDERTAKER'S IN ARCADIA. SHERIFF SCHMID
STANDS AT LEFT.

DALLAS PUBLIC LIBRARY, HAYES COLLECTION

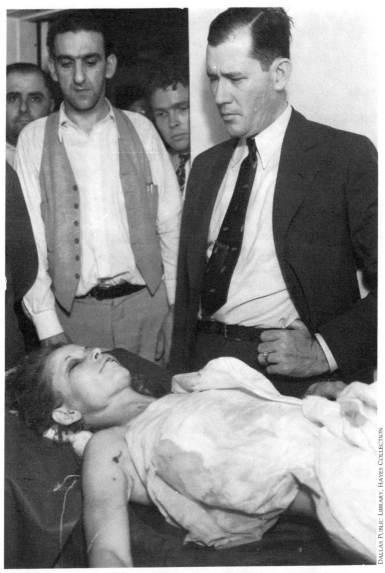

BONNIE AT THE UNDERTAKER'S IN ARCADIA. SHE AND CLYDE RECEIVED ABOUT 50 BULLETS APIECE. STANDING AT RIGHT IS BILL DECKER, CHIEF DEPUTY UNDER DALLAS COUNTY SHERIFF SMOOT SCHMID.

DALLAS PUBLIC LIBRARY, HAYES COLLECTION

out of the ditch and onto the road for the ride into Arcadia, the parish seat. The Louisiana officers led the way, Hamer and Gault drove behind them, and Alcorn and I followed behind the wrecker.

"Can't hear a damned thing," Alcorn shouted to me as I pulled my V-8 into the line of cars that soon would grow — believe it or not — to a two-hundred-car procession into Arcadia. I only half heard him and might not have heard at all if I hadn't been watching his mouth move. I held my nose as if to blow it, and it helped some in getting the ringing to stop.

It was a silent ride, keeping just behind the wrecker, seeing the holes in the tan car, holes we put there, and seeing the reddened top of Clyde's head as his corpse was leaned over the wheel just ahead of me. It's not the most pleasant ride a man can have on an otherwise bright May morning. The day was already sticky and hot, and the salt from the sweat that beaded on my forehead stung the raw flesh on my face that the insects had left during the awful last two sleepless days and nights.

We were nearing the Arcadia community and already I didn't like the looks of what was happening. Suddenly the wrecker stopped dead. It couldn't have happened in a worse place: on the road, opposite a schoolhouse.

The attraction was simply too much for the youngsters. They flew to the car to view the grisly sights until Alcorn leaped out of our car to try to order them away. Despite everything he could do, they already had plucked frayed strands from Bonnie's red dress, ripped samples of her hair, smeared their little fingers in clumps of not-yet-coagulated blood. In a short time, but not soon enough to prevent the spectacle from developing before the eyes of schoolchildren, the wrecker driver got his truck moving again.

Arcadia was filling up. The little town was the destination of reporters from all over the country now. But as we were arriving, like conquerers with some macabre trophy, I didn't feel at all like a conquerer. The wrecker first stopped in front of a furniture store; Congers Funeral Home was in the rear of it. The bodies of Clyde and Bonnie were removed from the car and placed on tables in a small room inside. We had to push the crowds back to get them inside. The car was left on exhibit, and the street filled with gawkers.

I felt a sense of relief that it was all over, a duty done, nothing more than that, nothing heroic so far as I was concerned.

But the crowds were pushing past me, driven by some strange drive to see the young lovers laid out on the slab. A line formed, and the push to get inside the funeral parlor in back of the furniture store was on before the undertaker had time even to clean them up.

I felt sick all over. It hadn't bothered me at the time. I had held up fairly well through the sleepless nights and sticky hot days. The shooting itself, there was not all that much to that; I had expected to have fear, but I had contained it, as the other officers had contained their fears when the instant came for the ambush. I really was having a reaction. I shook. Alcorn, too, was shaking like a leaf; here was a strong and able officer who had been in gunfights before, and he was shaking. I felt that I would throw up, but there was nothing to throw up.

I pushed my way out of the furniture parlor to the outside air, through the crowd that I thought had gone insane. A woman kissed me. I said "What's that for?" She said she was Sophie Stone, the home economist from Ruston or someplace who had been kidnapped once by Clyde and Bonnie. I remembered about that. But I had to get outside. People were tearing at the car, plucking away shards of glass, pinching off pieces of upholstery. Almost mechanically, I rushed to it to save it from destruction. After all, even in its condition, the car belonged to someone up in Kansas who had reported it stolen, and he was entitled to have it back. I glanced inside, through a shattered window glass, to the shredded interior lining of what had been almost a new car when Barrow got hold of it less than a month ago.

The wrecker moved the car away to the garage, where it could be unhooked. And now when we decided it should be moved behind a steel wire fence, the car started on its own power — and it was driven away, through a mob that kept it surrounded all the way. And even when it was put behind the fence, crowds strained against it to get a closer look.

REPRINTED WITH PERMISSION OF THE DALLAS TIMES HERALD.

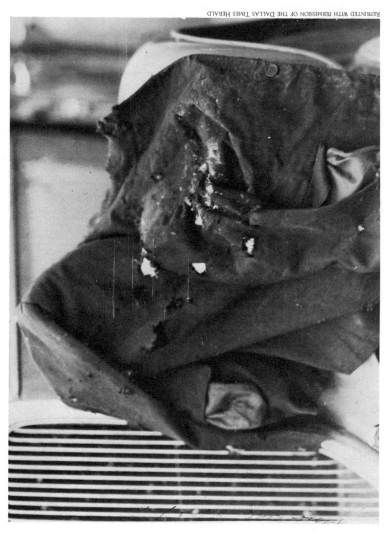

CLYDE'S BULLET-TORN COAT DRAPED ON THE FENDER OF HIS CAR.

DALLAS PUBLIC LIBRARY, HAYES COLLECTION

THE DEATH CAR WAS TAKEN TO THE JAIL YARD IN ARCADIA, WHERE A TEXAS HIGHWAY PATROLMAN (FAR LEFT) CAN HARDLY BELIEVE HIS EYES. NEXT TO HIM IS SHERIFF SCHMID; AT THE RIGHT OF THE CAR, WITH HIS ARM ON THE DOOR, IS FRANK HAMER.

185

"We need you over here for pictures," a photographer called, tugging at my shoulder. The idea struck me as absurd at the time. My clothes still were stained with blood, and my shirt bore flecks and blobs of red, and there still was blood on my hands. "Can I get a statement," the reporters were asking Alcorn and me. He shook his head and looked at the ground. I didn't have anything worth saying.

Hamer was in the center of a cluster of newsmen. "I hated to bust a cap on a woman," he was saying. "Especially a woman sitting down. But then I thought of those officers she killed so wantonly and . . ."

Hamer was being modest about everything, but the reporters seemed to ask him questions that invited a reply that made them believe he was agreeing with all they had said. Had he really killed fifty people? He said he never talked about all those things. In good time, Hamer would leave just the slightest hint that Old Man Methvin had been of immeasurable help. He didn't really say it, but he didn't deny the rumor when it had made the rounds and came to him by way of a question. Had there really been a deal with Methvin in exchange for the work Methvin did in putting Clyde and Bonnie on the spot? Hamer said he got a lot of help from many people, and he wasn't going to say what it was that Methvin did. "Some things," the big fellow said airily, "are just not the public's business to know."

I was certain, and so was Alcorn, that if Frank Hamer couldn't handle the situation nicely, no one could. The photographers insisted that we pose for pictures with Mr. Hamer, and we knew that Sheriff Schmid back in Dallas would have wanted us to be cooperative and let the world know that the Dallas sheriff's department was in on the kill. Smoot was on his way to Arcadia at that very moment.

Smoot was elated when he arrived late in the afternoon, and he brought news of rewards that were being collected by the state people down at Austin, and also privately in Dallas, and he said he knew of at least $26,000 that would be distributed around among the six of us who were in on the ambush. It seemed like a whole lot of money, and Alcorn said he'd believe it the very minute he got hold of some of it. I hoped it

REPRINTED WITH PERMISSION OF THE DALLAS TIMES HERALD

THE SIX OFFICERS WHO KILLED BONNIE AND CLYDE. LEFT TO RIGHT, STANDING: PRENTIS OAKLEY, TED HINTON, BOB ALCORN, MANNY GAULT; KNEELING: FRANK HAMER, HENDERSON JORDAN

wouldn't be like my first experience with reward money. After I'd had some luck bringing in the two Burkley brothers and after they cleared four murders, several hundred dollars in checks were turned over to me while some people made some grand speeches about me that almost made me blush. But all but one of the checks, for five dollars, bounced when I presented them at the bank. Alcorn explained to me when he was breaking me in about rewards: in times of great excitement, sentiment for rewarding law enforcement people runs very high. And the givers have more sentiment than money.

By nightfall, someone said Arcadia's population had swelled to around twelve thousand from its normal three thousand. Hordes streamed into the funeral home in back of the furniture store until Dr. James L. Wade said he'd have to go to work to get the bodies prepared for a return to Dallas. His report, made out with a lead pencil that became more blunted as he proceeded, made note of something like fifty-five bullet holes and glass cuts on Clyde and fifty-two on Bonnie. It made no mention of burn scars on Bonnie's legs — so the care that was given to her even as Clyde stayed on the run must have been adequate. When Bonnie received the burns in the car wreck near Wellington, Texas, the farm woman who had seen her was certain she would be permanently scarred. Wade noted a tattoo on Bonnie's right thigh — the names "Bonnie and Roy" — for Roy Thornton, whom she had married while she was still in her mid-teens and had failed to divorce officially when Thornton was sent to prison for a crime committed during one of their long separations. Below Bonnie's left knee were two other scars, reminders that someone had operated to remove a bullet put there in the ambush at Sowers, Texas, on November 23, 1933. Clyde also wore marks of tattoos that had already been noted in his police record: a "USN" for Navy, though he had never served in the Navy, and EBW — probably from a time when he was an apprentice car thief and was giving police his name as "Elvin Williams."

Some important business still surrounded the case. Billie Mace and Floyd Hamilton were being held in Fort Worth, charged with the slaying of the two officers on Easter Sunday at Grapevine. Alcorn and I were certain that the farmer whose

188

eyewitness account and identification from photographs of Billie and Floyd was mistaken; too much evidence pointed to Clyde and Bonnie and Henry Methvin. Ballistics tests on two of the guns found in the death car would exonerate Billie and Floyd, but this would take a while.

The news of the slaying made front pages all over the world. In the Southwest, and especially in Dallas, newspaper Extras! would sell like hotcakes. And stories were carrying the speculation that Irvin Methvin "set up Clyde and Bonnie" or "betrayed" them in exchange for leniency for Henry Methvin "even after Clyde had recently bought a farm for the Methvins," according to some accounts. But these did not worry me; I heard what people were saying about the newspaper stories, but I never read them.

Sheriff Schmid filled me in on some of the other reaction that greeted the news of the death of Clyde and Bonnie. W. D. Jones, who had turned on them after his many adventures, had said "he wasn't sad or he wasn't glad either" about the deaths, but he felt he was "free again, because they won't come and kill me."

Mrs. E. M. Stamps, out in Carlsbad, New Mexico, an aunt, was quoted in the papers as saying she felt safer because she had been "living in fear" Clyde would come and take revenge on her for calling the law on them when they came to visit. In the Jefferson City, Missouri, prison, Buck's widow, Blanche, was quoted as saying, "It's probably the best thing that they both died together."

But the parents and brothers and sisters of Clyde and Bonnie felt grief just as you would, or I would, if one in our family had been killed. They were broken up about it, even though they were certain it was going to end the way it did.

Clyde's dad, Henry Barrow, went to Arcadia to accompany the body of his boy back to Dallas. Henry seldom had left his filling station to go on the secret meetings with Clyde and Bonnie. Even when someone would pick up Cumie to take her to meet secretly somewhere near Dallas with Clyde and Bonnie, Henry would stay and mind the store.

But this man who had seldom showed emotion before came to identify his boy at the Arcadia funeral home and was broken up with grief. He sat in a rocking chair in the furniture store part of the building, his gray head bowed in his hands, and he constantly wiped tears from his red-lined eyes. To lose both Buck and Clyde in less than a year weighed heavy on his head.

As for Alcorn and me, we were thankful to get back to Dallas — though the home-town people showed the same morbid tendencies to crowd the funeral homes where the bodies of Clyde and Bonnie were put on display. At home, having a chance to see my wife and baby boy again was satisfaction enough for me. Still, the ugly scenes of mobs pushing for a look at the bodies lingered with me.

Would Clyde and Bonnie be buried ''side by side'' as Bonnie had promised in her poem they would? They would not. Her mother, Mrs. Emma Parker, would have no part of that. ''Clyde had her for two years and look what it did to her,'' she said. And the Barrows did not insist; Clyde would be laid to rest at sundown Friday, alongside his brother, Buck, so recently buried on a windswept hill in West Dallas.

In postponing Bonnie's funeral until the following day, the Parker family had hopes that Billie Mace would be freed of murder charges in Fort Worth and would be allowed to attend. We had hurried to get the guns to the Remington Arms man, so the ballistics tests could be made on guns that would prove Clyde's part in the shooting, but the report wouldn't be back for another few days.

From the time Clyde's body was put on display at Sparkman-Holtz-Brand Chapel, mobs outside were allowed to file past his open casket and have a look. ''Otherwise, we'll never get them to disperse,'' said the funeral home director. ''They've torn up all my shrubbery, all my lawn.''

Late into the night Thursday and most of Friday, the curious crowds came, many children among them, more women than men, to ogle and to say they saw. The official guess was that thirty thousand viewed Clyde's body at Sparkman, and about forty thousand passed by Bonnie's casket at McKamy-Campbell.

A columnist in the *Dallas Times Herald* wrote of the hysteria and morbid curiosity that gripped otherwise upstanding people in the wake of the ambush that finished Bonnie and Clyde:

"Indicative of the general hysteria was the visit to the Barrow bier by that eminent comedian of the screen, Mr. Bert Wheeler. In town for a short stay, he joined the mob which fought to pay Barrow homage. On being recognized by the simpering sillies in the crowd, Mr. Wheeler consented graciously to sign a few autographs, but even this live personality could not divert long the adoration of the public for a dead killer.

"Stemming from this blanket sentiment has been development of widespread resentment against officers who stamped out the terrors of this section . . . and at one of the country clubs where the elite gathered, the feeling was voiced on all sides that Hamer and Hinton, Alcorn and the others were 'cowardly murderers . . .' "

Clyde's last rites attracted all the crude misbehavior that could accompany a funeral. Crowds pushed and shoved to get into the Sparkman-Holtz-Brand Chapel service, which was meant to be private for family and friends. I attended, for I counted many of the Barrow family my friends. But many who couldn't get inside stood outside and cracked crude jokes, and some snickering greeted the comforting remarks that the Reverend Clifford Andrews of the Gospel Lighthouse spoke to the family. As the preacher read the fourteenth chapter of Job and a quartet began singing "I Need Thee Every Hour," Mrs. Barrow could be heard sobbing for her boy. The snickers of the crowd outside punctuated both song and sobbing. And it was then that Henry Barrow lost his composure; he looked like a broken man who wanted to lash out against the taunts of the mob. But he merely cried as he followed the coffin to the waiting hearse for the ride to the cemetery.

And even there, the grave had been cut too wide. When the crowd pressed forward to get a better view as the casket was lowered, the crush almost pushed the front-row family members right into the open grave. Mercifully, it was over quickly. The crowd began to disperse as the first spades of earth were thrown on the casket. A low-flying plane dropped a huge bouquet that landed nearby.

Compared with the funeral for Clyde, Bonnie's rites were a model of decorum. About 150 family and friends crowded the chapel of McKamy-Campbell Funeral Home on Forest Avenue in South Dallas and heard the Reverend Andrews say he loved Bonnie "though I never knew her" and "to help her now is a privilege."

There were only minor disturbances among the three hundred who came to the funeral chapel, pressing against the restraining ropes and waiting outside for a glance at the family arriving and departing for the procession to the Fishtrap Cemetery in West Dallas.

Billie Mace, Bonnie's sister, arrived under escort, and she was permitted to attend the funeral before returning to the Tarrant County jail. The heavily emotional time was too much. She fainted as she saw Bonnie's face covered with a filmy white veil in the open casket. She was revived. But after the services, Bonnie's mother also fainted and was barely conscious as she was carried to the car from the chapel while a male quartet sang "Lord, Abide With Me."

At the cemetery the largest wreath on Bonnie's casket was placed there by the newsboys. They were, in the end, among the few who had benefited by the short and violent life of the young lovers who had been separated only in death. Since Wednesday, one report in a Dallas newspaper had it, newsboys had sold 490,000 extra papers, about three times their regular sale.

The weeks passed, and so did the phobia and hysteria. The reward money finally came and I remember the sum I got, the same as Alcorn's — $200.23.

The expense voucher we turned in for the final six weeks of our search was $571.50, broken down this way: hotels, $120 (for we seldom used them); meals, $138; gas and oil, $305; drayage for pulling a car, $8.50.

Alcorn and I were put on other cases, and we continued to be praised by some and criticized by others for the way we helped to end the saga of Clyde and Bonnie. In time, I learned there was nothing I could do to change it either way.

It was all over, and yet it was not. Clyde and Bonnie had blazed their names across the Southwest, and they went down as they had lived, together. But there were many, dead and alive, whose lives they had touched, and mine was only one.

Henry Methvin, whose father was accused (actually wrongly) of putting Clyde and Bonnie on the spot, was one of more than twenty people who were tried for harboring Clyde and Bonnie — federal charges. Along with Methvin, many other people received sentences — even the mothers of the fugitives — for not turning them in to authorities. Thirty-day sentences were meted out to Mrs. Cumie Barrow, Mrs. Emma Parker, and Raymond Hamilton's mother, Mrs. Steve Davis. Others received up to two years.

It was much later, when the sentences were finally passed, that one of the giants of Southwest law enforcement, U.S. Marshal Red Wright, inquired whether I would take a few of those who had harbored Bonnie and Clyde to scattered prisons. With all respect to Marshal Wright, I begged off; I didn't believe it was right at all.

W. D. Jones was convicted for his part in the murder of Tarrant County deputy Malcolm Davis when he accompanied Clyde and Bonnie; he received fifteen years.

Methvin served ten years in the Oklahoma prison but never was brought to trial for offenses in Texas. After winning his freedom, he operated a restaurant near a war plant for a time in Minden, Louisiana, and was struck down and killed by a train in the late 1940s. His father, Irvin Methvin, who wanted the best for his son but never sold out his son's fugitive companions, died without anyone except six officers knowing the real truth of what he did.

In time, one by one, my companions on the ambush in Louisiana all died — or I would not even now relate the real story of Irvin Methvin's "kidnapping" for use as bait in one of the century's most famous ambush shootings.

The parents of Bonnie and Clyde are gone now, too. But several of their relatives, sisters and brothers, have been my long-time friends.

A story that must be included in any retelling of the saga of Bonnie and Clyde is the part played by Raymond Hamilton. He had written that he "couldn't keep up with Clyde's pace." But he almost did.

On the day Clyde and Bonnie died in Louisiana, Hamilton was waiting in the Denton County jail for transfer again to Huntsville prison — this time with 362 years hanging over his head in sentences. He was tried once more, at Crockett, for the death of the prison guard, Major Crowson, when Bonnie and Clyde helped Hamilton and Joe Palmer and others break out of Eastham Prison Farm. The state was determined: despite Hamilton's plea that he would gladly spend the rest of his life in Alcatraz if the state wouldn't ask the death penalty, Hamilton was sentenced to die in the electric chair.

Again he broke out of prison — though, in fact, it was all engineered for him. And eight months later I was in a group that captured him again — without firing a shot. The prison system didn't let him get away this time. Joe Palmer was captured, too. One after the other on the same night in 1935, they died in the electric chair.

There is much more to the story, but perhaps this is where I should end it. After forty-two years, people still are inquisitive about Clyde and Bonnie and want to know more about them, and I continue to be asked how they came to be whatever they came to be.

I thought I understood them as well as any man. I never joined those who said they were "mad-dog killers"; I never called Clyde Barrow a "punk," as others who knew him less well had called him. I never tried to defend what they did, nor to defend them. But I understood, even at the time, how they piled murder upon murder: once they knew, beyond the shadow of a doubt, that capture could only mean death in the electric chair, they resisted capture — and sometimes they resisted by killing their would-be captors. They could continue this way only so long, until they would die. They stuck together, and they loved each other. That just about tells it.

Appendix A — People Killed by the Barrow Gang

Year	Date	Name	Occupation	Place
1932	Apr. 23	J. N. Bucher	storekeeper	Hillsboro, Texas
	Aug. 5	E. C. Moore	deputy sheriff	Atoka, Oklahoma
	Oct. 11	Howard Hall	butcher	Sherman, Texas
	Dec. 5	Doyle Johnson	lumber salesman	Temple, Texas
1933	Jan. 6	Malcolm Davis	deputy sheriff	Dallas, Texas
	Apr. 13	J. W. Harryman	constable	Joplin, Missouri
		Harry McGinnis	detective	Joplin, Missouri
	June 23	Henry D. Humphrey	city marshal	Alma, Arkansas
1934	Jan. 16	Major Crowson	prison guard	Eastham, Texas
	Apr. 1	E. B. Wheeler	Highway Patrolman	Grapevine, Texas
		H. D. Murphy	Highway Patrolman	Grapevine, Texas
	Apr. 6	Cal Campbell	constable	Commerce, Oklahoma

Appendix B

Chronology:
The Career of Bonnie and Clyde

1909   Mar. 24   Clyde Barrow born, the fourth in a family of eight children, at a farm outside of Teleco, near Ennis, southeast of Dallas.

1910   Oct. 1   Bonnie Parker, second of three children, born to a bricklayer's family at Rowena, Texas. Moved to Cement City after death of father in 1914.

1922   Parents of Clyde Barrow move to Dallas when Clyde is thirteen; he attends Cedar Valley School until he is sixteen and in the seventh grade.

1926   Dec.   Clyde formally charged for first time, for auto theft; subsequently arrested five more times for suspected auto theft.

1930   Mar. 2   Clyde convicted in McLennan County Court (Waco) of seven counts of theft over fifty dollars (for separate burglaries and auto thefts) and sentenced to prison to serve two years for each count (total, fourteen years). Escapes jail (with help of Bonnie Parker, who smuggles gun inside his cell) but is arrested a short time later in Middletown, Ohio, and returned to Texas.

        Apr. 21   Clyde admitted to Texas State Penitentiary at Eastham Farm, Crockett, Texas.

1931   Dec. 27   Ivan (Buck) Barrow, older brother of Clyde Barrow, turns himself in to prison authorities at Huntsville, Texas; says he had escaped prison before and at the insistence of his wife, Blanche, has "decided to go straight, serve out my time."

196

1932	Jan. 27	Clyde Barrow, attempting to get assignment away from the prison farm at Eastham, has a fellow prisoner cut off two of his toes with an ax.
	Feb. 8	Governor Ross Sterling signs parole papers, freeing Clyde Barrow from prison. Clyde returns home to Dallas and rejoins his sweetheart, Bonnie Parker. Later in the same month, Clyde goes to Worcester, Massachusetts, to take job with a construction crew, but stays only a few weeks before returning to Dallas.
	Mar. 25	Clyde Barrow and Raymond Hamilton hold up manager of Sims Oil Company in Dallas.
	Apr. 23	Clyde Barrow and Raymond Hamilton hold up J. N. Bucher's station/store on outskirts of Hillsboro, Texas. As Bucher is opening his safe, gun discharges and bullet ricochets and kills him.
	July 16	Bookkeeper Roy Evans of the Palestine Ice Company in East Texas is beaten and robbed by two bandits whose descriptions fit Clyde and Ray.
	July 27	First State Bank of Willis, Texas, in Montgomery County robbed by two young bandits who take more than three thousand dollars and lock bank manager and cashier in a safe. This job is later traced to Clyde and Ray.
	July 29	Bandits identified as Raymond Hamilton and Clyde Barrow rob Interurban Rail Station keeper C. H. Spears at Grand Prairie.
	Aug. 1	Hamilton and Clyde Barrow rob Neuhoff Packing Company plant offices in daring daylight caper and escape with almost five hundred dollars.
	Aug. 5	Clyde Barrow, Bonnie Parker, and Raymond Hamilton visit a roadside dance hall at Stringtown, near Atoka, Oklahoma. When they are asked to vacate a car they have been sitting in, gunfire erupts and Deputy Sheriff E. C. Moore falls dead; Sheriff C. G. Maxwell is seriously wounded. Hamilton, Barrow, and Bonnie Parker escape in a series of stolen cars.

	Aug. 16	While Clyde, Bonnie, and Ray are stopping off at the home of Bonnie's aunt, Mrs. Millie Stamps, outside Carlsbad, New Mexico, Deputy Sheriff Joe Johns comes to house to investigate ownership of the car that the three drove through town. Clyde brandishes shotgun, orders Johns inside the car, and they kidnap him. Johns is freed at San Antonio, Texas, the next day, and kidnap charges are filed in Carlsbad.
	Aug. 30	Clyde and Bonnie and Raymond Hamilton shoot way out of a roadblock prepared to stop them at Colorado River outside Wharton, Texas. A lawman is wounded. ''Assault to murder'' charges are added to the charges already filed against the fugitives.
	Oct. 8	Clyde Barrow and Raymond Hamilton rob bank of Cedar Hill, south of Dallas, and take $1,401 from assistant cashier R. H. Carroll. After the robbery, Hamilton parts company with Barrow and Bonnie Parker and joins Gene O'Dare in a trip to Michigan.
	Oct. 11	Clyde Barrow and Bonnie Parker hold up Little's Grocery in Sherman, Texas, and kill sixty-seven-year-old butcher Howard Hall when Hall attempts to thwart Barrow's escape.
	Dec. 5	With sixteen-year-old W. D. Jones, Clyde and Bonnie attempt to steal a car belonging to Doyle Johnson, salesman, at Temple, Texas. When Johnson discovers the young Jones at the wheel, he rushes out and attempts to thwart the crime. Clyde fires a pistol blast and Johnson slumps over dead.
	Dec. 6	Raymond Hamilton and Gene O'Dare are arrested by officers in Bay City, Michigan, at a roller-skating rink and are ordered back to Texas to stand trial for a series of crimes.
1933	Jan. 1	Smoot Schmid assumes office as Dallas County sheriff; among the new deputies hired by Schmid is Ted Hinton.

Jan. 6	Deputy Sheriff Malcolm Davis of Tarrant County (Fort Worth) is shot by Clyde Barrow, Bonnie Parker, and W. D. Jones as the three escape a police trap at Lillie McBride's house in West Dallas.
Jan. 25	Raymond Hamilton pleads not guilty at trial in District Court of Noland Williams in Dallas but offers no defense. Receives first of a series of sentences: thirty years for his part in robbery of Cedar Hill Bank and twenty-five years for robbery of Neuhoff Packing Company. (Trials continue throughout summer and terms totaling 362 years are assessed before Hamilton is transferred to Huntsville on August 8, 1933.)
Jan.	Motorcycle Officer Thomas Persell kidnapped and driven two hundred miles by Clyde and Bonnie and W. D. Jones before being freed at Poundstone Corner, Missouri.
Mar. 20	Buck Barrow is granted full pardon by Texas Governor Miriam (Ma) Ferguson. Leaves Huntsville on March 22 and returns to Dallas.
Apr. 13	Clyde and Buck Barrow, with Buck's wife, Blanche, and Bonnie Parker and W. D. Jones are caught in a stone bungalow in a residential section of Joplin, Missouri, by Missouri officers. When the fugitives fail to come out after officers call to them, gunfire erupts, killing Constable J. W. Harryman and Detective Harry McGinnis. The Barrow boys and W. D. Jones are less seriously wounded. Officers find a cache of film and evidence that Buck Barrow and his wife, Blanche, are with Clyde, Bonnie, and W.D.
Apr. 28	After stealing a car belonging to H. D. Darby in Ruston, Louisiana, the Barrow Gang is chased by Darby and a friend named Sophie Stone. When Darby and Miss Stone give up the case, the Barrows chase and kidnap them, driving to Waldo, Arkansas, before setting them free with five dollars ''to catch a bus home.''

June 10   Bonnie suffers serious burns when the Barrow car hurtles over an embankment west of Wellington, Collingsworth County, in the Texas Panhandle. When she is cared for at a farmhouse, Sheriff George T. Corry and Wellington Town Marshal Tom Hardy come to investigate. They are forced back inside their police car and kidnapped by the Barrow Gang. After a three-hour ride they are left tied to a tree outside Erick, Oklahoma.

June 19   Clyde Barrow eludes capture by Ted Hinton as he drives to Dallas to pick up Bonnie's sister, Billie, and bring her to Bonnie, who is severely burned. On the following day, Billie and Clyde return to the group outside Fort Smith, Arkansas, to help nurse Bonnie back to health.

June 23   Jones and one or both of the Barrows — Buck later confesses that he was the assailant, but many doubt it — engage officers in a gunfight, and Marshal Henry D. Humphrey is shot to death near Alma, Arkansas.

July 19   Clyde and Bonnie, along with Buck and Blanche Barrow and W. D. Jones, engage officers in a gun battle at Platte City, Missouri, and two officers are wounded. Buck Barrow is severely wounded; Blanche Barrow suffers serious eye wound.

July 23   Posse of lawmen surrounds the Barrow Gang and Buck is fatally wounded; he and Blanche are captured. Clyde is wounded — but he escapes with Bonnie and W. D. Jones after they swim a river and take a car at gunpoint at Dexter, Iowa.

July 29   Buck dies in hospital at Perry, Iowa.

July 31   Buck buried in West Dallas Cemetery after brief services at Sparkman-Holtz-Brand Chapel in Dallas.

Aug. 8   Raymond Hamilton transferred from Dallas to Huntsville, Texas, to begin serving prison terms totaling 362 years.

Nov. 8	Clyde and Bonnie rob office of McMurray Refinery at Arp, Texas, at gunpoint.
Nov. 15	W. D. Jones arrested in Houston. The next day, under interrogation by Officers Bob Alcorn and Ted Hinton, Jones claims he was an ''unwilling participant'' in escapades of Clyde and Bonnie and that he was held against his will.
Nov. 23	Clyde and Bonnie evade Ted Hinton, Bob Alcorn, Ed Caster, and Smoot Schmid, Dallas County officers who attempt to ambush them at the Sowers community northwest of Dallas.

1934	Jan. 11 to Jan. 16	James Mullen, newly released from Eastham Prison Farm, arranges with Floyd Hamilton and Clyde Barrow to free Raymond Hamilton from Eastham Farm. In the break on January 16, prison guard Major Crowson is killed. Along with Hamilton are escapees Joe Palmer, Henry Methvin, Hilton Bybee, and J. B. French. French and Bybee go their own ways and shortly afterward are captured. Palmer and Methvin continue to travel with Clyde, Bonnie, and Ray.
	Feb. 19	Clyde and Ray burglarize National Guard Armory at Ranger, Texas, providing supply of automatic weapons for future outlawry.
	Feb. 26	Clyde and Ray rob Lancaster, Texas, Bank. Later, division of the money causes split in their friendship.
	Mar. 6	Ray and his girl friend, Mary O'Dare, leave the Barrow Gang at Terre Haute, Indiana, and strike out on their own after bitter dispute with Clyde.
	Mar. 10	Clyde and Bonnie (accompanied by Methvin and Palmer) hold reunion with their mothers at a cemetery in Lancaster, south of Dallas. Such reunions occur periodically throughout the two years they are on the run from police. During this week Clyde is spotted by Ted Hinton but Hinton cannot shoot for fear of injuring bystanders.

Mar. 19	Raymond and Floyd Hamilton and truck driver John Basden rob Grand Prairie Bank of fifteen hundred dollars. Hamilton writes letter to Dallas Assistant District Attorney Winter King disclaiming any association with Clyde Barrow. He signs it with his fingerprint.
Mar. 31	Raymond Hamilton, with Mary O'Dare waiting outside, robs the only bank in the small Czech community of West, in Central Texas, and gets twelve hundred dollars. When his car skids into a bar ditch south of town, Hamilton kidnaps Mrs. Cam Gunter of Mexia, Texas, with her four-year-old son when they stop to offer help. The victims are freed unharmed early the next day in Houston.
Apr. 1	Clyde, with Bonnie and Henry Methvin, waits at an old meeting place near Grapevine, Texas (probably to meet and kill Ray Hamilton, who is expected to arrive there. Joe Palmer by this time has left Clyde and Bonnie and is a running mate of Hamilton). Ray does not show up, but when Highway Patrolmen E. B. Wheeler and H. D. Murphy approach on motorcycles, they are shot and killed — probably by Methvin and Bonnie as well as Clyde.
Apr. 3	Frank Hamer and Manny Gault, on special assignment from Prison Director Lee Simmons, join Ted Hinton and Bob Alcorn in search of Bonnie and Clyde.
Apr. 4	Clyde and Bonnie are sighted on busy street in Durant, Oklahoma, by the four officers. To protect the safety of bystanders, no shots are exchanged.
Apr. 5	Clyde, Bonnie, and Methvin are sighted in Texarkana, Arkansas.
Apr. 6	In Miami, Oklahoma, Constable Cal Campbell is fatally shot by Clyde Barrow as he approaches to investigate the Barrow car that is stuck in a muddy road. Chief of Police Percy Boyd is kidnapped and later freed at Fort Scott, Kansas. Boyd

reports that the fugitives carry an arsenal of weapons, and Bonnie is displeased at publicity that she smokes cigars.

Apr. 25   Ray Hamilton and a youth named T. R. Brooks hold up Lewisville, Texas, Bank and flee with six hundred dollars. They are captured outside of Howe, in Grayson County, near Sherman in North Texas.

Apr. 27   Clyde writes letter ridiculing his former running mate Hamilton for giving up without a fight. (In 1935, Raymond Hamilton escapes from prison and is recaptured by a group of officers that includes Ted Hinton. Joe Palmer is also captured, and the two die on the same night in the electric chair.)

May 23   Clyde Barrow and Bonnie Parker are killed in an ambush laid for them on a lonely road near Gibsland, Louisiana. Members of the posse are Bob Alcorn and Ted Hinton of the Dallas County sheriff's department; Frank Hamer and Manny Gault, on special assignment for Lee Simmons of the Texas prison system; and Louisiana officers Henderson Jordan, sheriff at Arcadia, and deputy Prentis Oakley. The shooting occurs at 9:15 A.M. When the bodies are examined at Arcadia, twenty miles east of Gibsland, a coroner says each has been hit ''more than 50 times.'' Counting both entry and exit penetrations, the car bears 167 holes according to a count at the time.

Index

Alcorn, Bob: ambush, final, ix, 157–186 *passim;* deputy sheriff, 27–28; encounters, with Clyde and Bonnie, 129–132, 138–139, with W. D. Jones, 100–103, with Buck Barrow, 78; first ambush, 104–107; and Ted Hinton, 49, 55, 100, 109, 111, 192; Joplin aftermath, 38–39, 47; mechanic, 132; posse, 134–135, 142; reward money, 188, 192

Allbright, George, 75

Allen, J. E., 142

Alma (Arkansas) bank, robbery of, 55

Ambush: final, ix, 157–172 *(see also* Cover-up); first, 103–105

Ammunition: Browning Automatic Rifle (B.A.R.), 37, 57, 64; Clyde Barrow's guns, 71–72, 102, 107, 123, 143, 170–171, 173; Ted Hinton's guns, 104, 111–112, 132, 157

Andrews, Reverend Clifford, 191–192

Arcadia, Louisiana, 161–189 *passim*

Arp, Texas, 97

Atoka, Oklahoma, 19

Bailey, Harvey, 89–94

Baker, Lincoln, 62

Barnes, George Kelly. *See* Kelly, Machine Gun

Barrow, Blanche Caldwell, 35–36, 48, 53–55, 189; "Blythe," 78; captured, 73; incidents, at Dexfield, 69–74, at Joplin, 36–39, in Platte City, 61–65; testimony and sentence, 77–80; wounded, 65, 68–69

Barrow boys, 8–9, 14

Barrow, Buck, 29, 35–36, 48, 77–78, 102; and Clyde Barrow, 36, 78, 80; captured, 73; death, 77, 79; early life, 7–9; funeral, 80–81; incidents, at Dexfield, 69–74, at Joplin, 36–39, at Platte City, 61–65; wounded, 65, 68–69, 72

Barrow, Clyde: alias Elvin Williams, 11, 188; ambush and death, 164–171, 173; axes toes, 12–13; and Buck Barrow, 8–9, 17, 35–36, 78–80, 190; car accident, 50–54; cars, 107, 108, 111, 144, 154; coroner's report, 179, 188; driving, 10, 20–22, 128, 131, 168; early life, 7–11, 196; employment, xii, 11, 14; family, meetings with, 53, 103, 124, 128–129, 146–147; first ambush, 103–105; first murder, 16–18; funeral, 189–192; habits, xiii, 13, 20, 76, 99, 115; and Raymond Hamilton, 14, 23, 28–29, 30–34, 118–119; Raymond Hamilton, estrangement from, 125, 127–128, 133, 135–137, 151–152, 156; and Ted Hinton, 49–50, 54, 103, 112–113, 128–132, 139, 162; incidents, at Dexfield, 69–75, at Joplin, 36–39, at Platte City, 61–65; in jail, 10–12; and W. D. Jones, 25, 101–103; letters, to Henry Ford, 154–155, to Raymond Hamilton, 151–154, to Winter King, 155–156; and Henry Methvin, 136, 158; Bonnie Parker, relationship with, xii, 7, 10, 13–15, 17–18, 54, 106, 123–127; paroled, 12–13, 18; public reaction to death, 179–190 *passim;* record when Hinton joined sheriff's office, 28; refusal to give up, 17–18, 100, 104, 131, 143, 151,

Love, John, 70
Luther, J. T., 84

McBride, Mrs. Lillie, 31–34, 101, 116
McGinnis, Harry, 37–38
McKamy-Campbell Funeral Home, 190, 192
McLennan County, Texas, 10, 151
McMurray Refinery, robbery of, 97–99

Mace, Billie, 54–57, 79, 124, 192; mistakenly identified as Bonnie Parker, 138, 147–148, 188–190
Machine Gun Kelly, xiii, 89–94
Manion, Tom, 93–95
Maxwell, C. G., 19
Methvin, Henry: and Clyde Barrow, 136–139, 141, 144, 146–147, 151; cover-up, 171, 178, 189; death, 193; Eastham Prison Farm breakout and aftermath, 119–128 *passim;* home, 138, 159, 161; separated from Clyde and Bonnie, 158–159, 162
Methvin, Irvin, 159–168, 171–172, 178, 186–189, 193
Miami, Oklahoma, 140, 142, 154
Middleton, Ohio, 10
Minden, Louisiana, 161, 164, 193
Minyard, Eck, 4
Moody, Governor Dan, 11
Moore, E. C., 19, 28
Mount Ayr, Iowa, 68–70
Mount Lebanon, Louisiana, 159, 162
Mullen, James, 116–119, 122, 125, 146–147, 150
Murders: J. N. Bucher, 16, 28, 30, 151; Cal Campbell, 140–143, 154; Major Crowson, 119, 150, 194; Malcolm Davis, 31–32, 101, 116, 193; Howard Hall, 23–24, 28; J. W. Harryman, 37–38; Henry D. Humphrey, 55–57; Doyle Johnson, 25, 28, 101–102; Harry McGinnis, 37–38; E. C. Moore, 19, 28; H. D. Murphy, 137–138, 147–148; E. B. Wheeler, 137–138,

147–148
Murphy, H. D., 137–138, 147–148

Nash, Frank, 89
Neuhoff Packing Company, robbery of, 18
New Orleans, Louisiana, 147–148

Oak Cliff, Texas, 3, 138
Oakley, Prentis M., 162–173, 178
O'Dare, Gene, 23, 29–30, 123
O'Dare, Mary, 23, 123–128, 133–136, 147–150
Oronogo (Missouri) bank, robbery of, 24–25

Paddock, L. R., 18
Palmer, Joe, 135, 146, 150–153, 157; Eastham Prison Farm breakout and aftermath, 118–128 *passim;* execution, 194
Parker, Billie Jean. *See* Mace, Billie
Parker, Bonnie: ambush and death, 164–171, 173; American Cafe, 10, 14, 21; Clyde Barrow, relationship with, xiv, 7, 10, 13–15, 17, 127; car accident and subsequent burns, 50–55, 58–69; cigar-smoking legend, xiii, 39, 47, 143; coroner's report, 188; early life, 8, 142, 145, 196; family, meetings with, xv, 101, 124, 128, 131, 146–147; first ambush, 104–105; funeral, 190, 192; habits, 76, 126; and Raymond Hamilton, 116–127, 135; and Ted Hinton, xiii–xiv, 7–8, 113–114, 130–131, 139, 169–170; incidents, at Atoka, 19, at Carlsbad, 21–22, at Dexfield, 69–75, at Grapevine, 136–138, at Joplin, 36–38, at Platte City, 61–65; jailed, 15; and W. D. Jones, 25, 74–75, 101–103, 158–162; letters written for Clyde, 36, 151–154; and Billie Mace, 54–57, 138; poem, xv–xvii, 173, 190; public reaction to death, 179–190 *passim;* and Roy Thornton, 8, 60, 188;

209

wounded, 74. *See also* Kidnappings; Murders; Robberies

Parker, Emma, 14, 79, 101, 113, 124, 146; arrested, 193; Bonnie's burns, 53–54; Bonnie's funeral, 190, 192

Parker family, 100, 124, 126, 155, 189

Parker Family Archives, xv

Parkland Hospital, 82, 84

Penn, Henry, 70

Perry, Iowa, 69–79 *passim*

Pitts, Barney, 148, 150

Pitts, Mary. *See* O'Dare, Mary

Platte City, Missouri, incident at, 61–67

Pleasant Mound, Texas, 82, 86

Poteau (Oklahoma) bank, robbery of, 126

Poundstone Corner, Missouri, 199

Pretty Boy Floyd, xiii, 51, 92

Prince, Kathryne, 81–86

Pritchards (farmer and his wife who helped Barrow Gang), 51–52

Pritchard, Mrs., 51–52

Ranger (Texas) National Guard Armory, robbery of, 123, 147

Reed Springs, Missouri, incident at, 125–126

Reich, Paul, 106–107

Reward money, 186, 192

Rhodes, Dusty, 31

Riley, Rags, 72

Robberies: George Allbright, 75; Alma (Arkansas) Bank, 55; Durant (Oklahoma) bank, 126; Enid (Oklahoma) National Guard Armory, 57, 60, 69; Fayetteville (Arkansas) Piggly-Wiggly groceries, 55–56; Fort Dodge (Iowa) filling stations, 60; Galena (Kansas), First National Bank of, 126; Grand Prairie (Texas) bank, 134, 136, 150; Grapevine (Texas), Home Bank of, 30–33; Lancaster (Texas) Bank, 122–126, 153; Lewisville (Texas), First State Bank of, 149–151; McMurray Refinery, 97–99; Neuhoff Packing Company, 18; Oronogo (Missouri) bank, 24–25; Perry (Iowa), sedan in, 69;

Poteau (Oklahoma) bank, 126; Ranger (Texas) National Guard Armory, 123, 147; Shiro (Texas) bank, 115; Sims Oil Company, 15–16; C. H. Spears, 18; West (Texas) bank, 136, 148, 150, 155; Willis (Texas), First State Bank of, 18

Rogers, Mrs. Frank, 57

Routon, Monroe, 115

Rowena, Texas, 8

Ruston, Louisiana, 47–49, 183

Saggau, Hugo, 76

Sailes, Louisiana, 162

Salyers, Deputy, 56, 78

San Antonio, Texas, 22

Schieffer, William, 137–138, 147

Schmid, Smoot, 4, 38, 99, 139; and Clyde Barrow, 129–130, 152; death of Clyde and Bonnie, 178, 186, 189; election as Dallas County Sheriff, 1, 5, 20, 27; first ambush, 104–105, 108–109; and Raymond Hamilton, 148, 150; and Ted Hinton, xii, 5, 33, 92, 134; and W. D. Jones, 103, 108; political pressure, 50, 86, 93–94, 104, 130, 133; posse, 134–135; and Lee Simmons, 116, 133–134; special assignment to Hinton, 95, 111

Schreider, Abe, 81, 87

Shannon, Armon, 91–92

Shannon, Mrs. Robert G., 90–92

Shannon, Robert G., 92

Sherman, Texas, 24, 149

Shiro (Texas) bank, robbery of, 115

Shreveport, Louisiana, 157, 161, 164

Simmons, Lee, 11, 116–117, 133–134, 172–178

Sims Oil Company, robbery of, 15–16

Sowers, Texas, incident at, 103–105, 111, 188

Sparkman-Holtz-Brand Chapel, 80, 190–191

Spears, C. H., 18

Spillers, Walter, 75

Stamps, Mrs. E. M., 21–22, 189

210